"From the training field to the b...
deep into the heart and soul of the ...
Christian is standing on the battlefield called life, and your only mission is to follow your leader—the Lord Jesus Christ."

JEFF STRUECKER, NATIONALLY KNOWN SPEAKER,
FORMER MEMBER OF TASK FORCE RANGER IN SOMALIA

"For Chuck Holton, a Ranger in the world's finest light infantry regiment, childhood faith became a manhood anchor. This *Pilgrim's Progress* in camouflage shows how a Christian young man grows to maturity through rigorous discipline. If you love Christ, you too will grow by this book. Spiritual maturity emerges out of the adversity of a soldier's life."

STU WEBER, BESTSELLING AUTHOR OF *TENDER WARRIOR*

"*This kid can write!* Chuck Holton leads the way to the ground level of combat in Panama and to the soaring heights of walking with Christ daily. You'll be inspired by how the Lord has led Chuck through the fiery trial of combat to serve today in his work and ministry. You'll want to read this book over and over, make your teenagers read it, and read it to your kids!"

JAMES BLACKWELL, MILITARY ANALYST TO THE PENTAGON,
CNN, AND FOX NEWS

"Chuck Holton draws on the values and character enhanced through tough, realistic Ranger training and the brotherhood of arms. He lived with a special code common to all Rangers—the Ranger Creed. At a time of life-threatening danger, the creed made the difference between success and failure. The vignettes in this book serve as an inspiration for all of life's challenges."

GENERAL WILLIAM F. "BUCK" KERNAN, RETIRED, FORMER SUPREME
ALLIED COMMANDER, ATLANTIC, AND COMMANDER IN CHIEF,
U.S. JOINT FORCES COMMAND

A MORE ELITE SOLDIER

CHUCK HOLTON

Multnomah® Publishers *Sisters, Oregon*

A MORE ELITE SOLDIER
published by Multnomah Publishers, Inc.

© 2003 by Charles W. Holton
International Standard Book Number: 1-59052-215-X

Cover image by Getty Images/Sean Murphy

Unless otherwise indicated, Scripture quotations are from:
The Holy Bible, New International Version © 1973, 1984 by International Bible Society, used
by permission of Zondervan Publishing House

Other Scripture quotations are from:
The Holy Bible, New Living Translation (NLT) © 1996. Used by permission of Tyndale
House Publishers, Inc. All rights reserved.

Multnomah is a trademark of Multnomah Publishers, Inc.,
and is registered in the U.S. Patent and Trademark Office.
The colophon is a trademark of Multnomah Publishers, Inc.

Printed in the United States of America

For information:
MULTNOMAH PUBLISHERS, INC. • P.O. BOX 1720 • SISTERS, OR 97759

Library of Congress Cataloging-in-Publication Data:

Holton, Chuck.
    A more elite soldier / By Chuck Holton.
        p. cm.
    ISBN 1-59052-215-X (pbk.)
    1. Holton, Chuck. 2. United States. Army—Commando troops.
3. Soldiers—United States—Biography. 4. Christian biography—United
States. I. Title.

BR1725.H645A3 2003
248.4—dc21

                                            2003007614

03 04 05 06 07 08—10 9 8 7 6 5 4 3 2 1 0

For my beloved children,
Kiernan, Mason, Nathan, Joey, and Amy.
May you learn to value purpose over pleasure,
duty over delight, and faith over feeling
in pursuit of the great adventure that God has for you.

Contents

THE RANGER
CREED

Recognizing that I volunteered as a Ranger, fully knowing the hazards of my chosen profession, I will always endeavor to uphold the prestige, honor, and high esprit de corps of my Ranger Regiment.

Acknowledging the fact that a Ranger is *a more elite soldier* who arrives at the cutting edge of battle by land, sea, or air, I accept the fact that as a Ranger my country expects me to move farther, faster, and fight harder than any other soldier.

Never shall I fail my comrades. I will always keep myself mentally alert, physically strong, and morally straight; I will shoulder more than my share of the task whatever it may be, one hundred percent and then some.

Gallantly will I show the world that I am a specially selected and well-trained soldier. My courtesy to superior officers, neatness of dress, and care of equipment shall set the example for others to follow.

Energetically will I meet the enemies of my country. I shall defeat them on the field of battle, for I am better trained and will fight with all my might. Surrender is not a Ranger word. I will never leave a fallen comrade to fall into the hands of the enemy, and under no circumstances will I ever embarrass my country.

Readily will I display the intestinal fortitude required to fight on to the Ranger objective and complete the mission, though I be the lone survivor.

LIFE IS COMBAT

Consume my life, my God, for it is Thine.
I seek not a long life but a full one, like you, Lord Jesus.

JIM ELLIOT

"Look at the nations and watch—and be utterly amazed.
For I am going to do something in your days that you would not believe,
even if you were told."

HABAKKUK 1:5

Have you ever felt the gut-wrenching shot of adrenaline that comes with sudden, mortal danger?

Have you ever endured an experience that was so stressful it made all of your problems up to that point seem like blessings in comparison?

Can you remember a time when you looked heavenward and asked, "Why me?"

Each one of us faces multiple stresses in our lives.

Overdue bills. Health concerns. Relationship worries. Family hassles. The pressures of school and work and too many responsibilities.

Then, on top of it all, tragedy thunders into your life. Crisis descends without warning.

What do you do when your walls are crumbling and too many troubles assault you all at once? Someone once said that facing troubles one at a time is one thing—it's when they run in packs that you get a little worried.

How do you respond? Do you freeze? Fight? Flee? Or do you learn something about yourself?

The story contained in these pages details many of the lessons I learned as a member of the U.S. Army's 75th Ranger Regiment. From training to combat, the challenge of becoming one of these elite soldiers is surpassed only by the rigors of actually *being* one. The trials I endured during my enlistment taught me much about myself, about life, and about God.

But this isn't meant to be a book about me. It's really about you.

Four years as a Ranger will redefine the words *high stress* for anyone. But you don't need to enlist in the Army to face the stress of combat. Everyday life can be tough enough to break anyone who isn't prepared.

Combat takes many forms, and you don't need to be shot at to experience it. Combat can be the loss of a loved one, a business failure, or a broken relationship. Whatever the crisis, times like these cause you to see your life in a whole new light—and begin to redefine what really matters.

In a very real sense, life *is* combat. It really doesn't matter what shape it takes. What matters is how you face it, how it changes you, and who you turn to for help.

Author Randy Alcorn writes, "No soldier wins a battle that he is not prepared for, and none prepares for a battle that he doesn't know exists."

This isn't just a battle against crushing time schedules, depressing personal finances, and domestic squabbles. It's a very real battle in the spiritual realm for your mind, your body, and—ultimately—your soul.

To avoid the battle or pretend that it has nothing to do with you is, in the end, more dangerous and painful than joining the fight. So the underlying question throughout this book is this: What kind of soldier will *you* be?

The stories you're about to read are true, though some of the names have been changed, and some of the details on different missions have been combined. It is my hope that within these pages you will see the parallels between life as a Ranger and the calling given to every follower of Christ—the call to become *a more elite soldier* in His service.

ON MISSION

There's so much that I haven't done that I want to do. So many things I haven't seen, been to, experienced. I'm anxious and excited! What's God got for me? It's like I'm standing on the edge of an ocean of possibilities. I can't see the other side, but I know it's great. I can't wait to cross, and I know that although there will always be the peaks and the troughs, every step is an adventure. Life is LIFE! Fill me to overflowing.

CHUCK HOLTON, AGE 15, JOURNAL ENTRY

"Get ready!"

The jumpmaster shouts over the roar of aircraft engines, stirring me from deep thought. It's almost 1 A.M. on December 20, 1989. I'm one of nearly one hundred Airborne Rangers who, four hours ago at Fort Benning, Georgia, packed into this C-130 transport plane—built to carry no more than sixty-four jumpers.

After serving in the Army for about two and a half years, I carry the rank of specialist. Tonight I can barely feel my legs. I am buried under an eighty-pound rucksack attached to my parachute harness at the waist, and overlapped by those of the Rangers packed tightly around me.

"Outboard personnel, stand UP!"

I look across at my friend Philip Lear, and he gives me a wry smile that says, *Here goes nothing!* I reach over and clasp his wrist, helping him struggle to his feet in the cramped confines of the aircraft—a near impossible task. Earlier this year, Lear and I were assigned as buddies in Ranger school, a two-month leadership course where we spent the majority of our time running patrols through every type of terrain imaginable.

It was wintertime, and many nights we had to huddle together for warmth. We've been through a lot together. Lear is like a brother to me. I wonder if it was God's intention that we ended up side-by-side on this airplane. He is with the Second Ranger Battalion, stationed at Fort Lewis, Washington; I am with the Third Battalion at Fort Benning, Georgia. This is the first we've seen of each other since the day we graduated from Ranger school ten months ago. I regret that we haven't been able to do much catching up on the ride down. The inside of a C-130 is definitely not conducive to conversation. Lear did tell me that he is engaged to be married. I hope to be able to talk to him sometime later and find out more. But once we hit the ground, we must go our separate ways, following separate platoons, accomplishing different jobs.

"Inboard personnel, stand UP!"

It's my turn to struggle to my feet. I can't believe it's gone this far. This mission may actually go down. We've been called up for real-life missions before, but they've always been canceled at the last minute.

This time our destination is Panama.

The overall mission is to arrest Panama's corrupt dictator, Manuel Noriega, and help establish a democratic government. Of course, Third Battalion's specific mission is much more limited in scope—we're simply the kickoff team. There are units at every U.S. base in Panama waiting for H-hour to come. Our coordinated attack should be swift and violent.

There's much we don't know about the political or strategic reasons for the mission, but it's gratifying to think that the Army might finally use us. We've been training for this operation for months. If I have to serve my entire enlistment training for combat without actually experiencing it, I will always wonder how I would have performed in battle. It would be like training for the Super Bowl and then never getting to play.

When I was a kid, I did yard work for an older gentleman who was a deacon in our church. He had been in the Airborne in World War II. His stories about parachuting into combat fascinated me, and I used to dream about what it would be like to do the same.

Tonight I might finally get to find out.

"Hook up!"

We all struggle to attach our static lines to the overhead cable that will pull our chutes open once we exit the aircraft. The task is made difficult by the fact that it's so crowded—we can hardly move. I wonder if our leaders planned it this way so that we will be anxious to jump. If they did, it's working. I am careful to check that my static line is securely fastened to the cable, though my faith in getting to the ground safely does not lie in the cable above me or the parachute on my back. If it did, I don't know that I would have ever made it through jump school to begin with.

"Check equipment!"

Time to focus. We're all deadly serious now. Girls, bills, and all the other problems that seem so important in my day-to-day life are nowhere in my consciousness at this moment. There isn't room in my head for them. One hundred percent of my faculties are intent on the job that we have to do here in Central America. We do our best to check each other's equipment in the dim light of the aircraft interior. I try to ensure that there's nothing under my feet that I might trip over when heading for the door. I can't even *see* my feet. A vice begins to tighten in my gut as my pulse quickens.

"Sound off for equipment check!"

Someone slaps me on the shoulder. I tap the guy in front of me and shout, "OK!" He taps the guy in front of him, and so on, toward the jumpmaster at the rear of the aircraft. Once the jump-master gets the "All OK" signal, he will open the aircraft door and begin spotting for the drop zone.

Behind me is Mike Bohannon, a brand-new private. He's only been up in an aircraft on nine occasions, and he's jumped every time. He doesn't know what it's like to land in an airplane. This will be his third jump with our unit; the other two he performed in train-ing for this occasion. I'm worried about him, because he's so new and because he's my responsibility. I lean back and yell in his ear, "When we hit the ground, stay put, and I'll come find you. Stick with me and you'll be OK!"

He nods, wide-eyed.

The white lights go out. They're about to open the door. To say that it's uncomfortable standing with an eighty-pound rucksack full of ammunition hanging between your legs is like saying Siberia is brisk in winter. My M-203 grenade launcher is in its case, strapped securely to my left side.

I review the mission in my head. We're jumping onto an airfield at a place called Rio Hato, about forty miles south of Panama City. Some of the most ruthless of the Panamanian defense forces (PDF) are housed there. We are to take the airfield and ensure that none of the PDF special forces, the *Macho de Monte,* have a chance to reinforce enemy positions in Panama City, where more Rangers are preparing to attack. My platoon's part in the mission is to take out a couple of anti-aircraft guns that border the runway. We are then to clear and occupy the buildings of a military school located on one side of the airfield. Intel says that the barracks are empty, their soldiers home for Christmas, so clearing the buildings shouldn't take long.

Murphy's Law, however, has a tendency to take over in these situations, so we are prepared for anything.

At least...I hope we are.

Suddenly, the roar of the night intensifies as the doors open. Hot, humid air floods in, reminding us that we aren't in Georgia anymore, where it was sleeting when we took off. Next to the door I can just see the red light that will soon turn green, signalling for us to jump. The jumpmaster takes hold of the door frame and leans far out into the night, looking for the airfield. All he sees is water. We are coming in over the Atlantic Ocean at five hundred feet. When we jump, there won't even be time to pull my reserve chute if the main one doesn't open. I'm not sure why I even wore one, except that it is simply part of the pre-jump checklist.

We stand for what seems like hours in the dim red light, sweating profusely and listening to the screaming engines. Not being able to talk leaves us alone with our thoughts.

Unaccountably, a quiet sense of peace settles over me.

I've been training for this moment since I first raised my hand at the swearing-in ceremony two and a half years earlier. Scared? Yes— but not so much about my safety. I'm more concerned about how I will perform once I hit the tarmac below. It's a natural feeling, I suppose, when you're about to parachute into a firefight in a foreign country from an aircraft traveling at one hundred and fifty knots.

Beyond all those conflicting emotions, however, I know this is where I'm supposed to be at this very moment. And I believe that if a person follows God's purpose for his life, there's no safer place to be.

I glance toward the window just in time to see two closely spaced flashes of light. There's no turning back now. The mission calls for two F-117 stealth fighter aircraft to drop five-hundred-pound bombs on the leading edge of the airfield to kick off the invasion. It's the first time these aircraft have ever been used in combat. The flashes confirm that the bombs have just detonated on the beach.

Game time.

A testosterone-filled "HOOAH!" goes up from the Rangers in our aircraft. We are first in line, with twelve more C-130s following, also packed with "death from above."

The jumpmaster screams, "Drop zone coming up!" I can't hear him, but I see his lips moving and know what he's saying. Lear reaches over and slaps me on the helmet. We shake hands. He gives me a thumbs-up that says, *Let's do this!*

I yell in his ear, "Be safe!" He nods and grins confidently.

The light turns green. Rangers start shuffling out the door as quickly as their much-encumbered state allows. For a long moment, those of us back toward the front of the aircraft aren't moving at all. Finally, enough guys have jumped to make room for us. Then we begin lumbering toward the open door, pulling our static lines along the overhead cable. Suddenly the C-130 starts banking sharply left, then right. The pilots are taking evasive action to avoid anti-aircraft fire. Now I *really* want out of this plane.

Everything around me moves in blurry slow motion, but my consciousness is razor sharp. At this second, my entire life is focused on this exact point in time. There is no past, no future, only present. The pre-game anxiety that I was feeling vanishes, leaving only white-hot, focused purpose. Ten feet from the door, the light turns red, signaling the end of the drop zone. The Air Force loadmaster steps up and tries to get us to stop jumping. Everyone ignores him. There's no way we're not jumping now. I run for the door and step into blackness....

I'm on mission.

1

THE DYING COCKROACH

Run in such a way as to get the prize.
Everyone who competes in the games goes into strict training.
They do it to get a crown that will not last;
but we do it to get a crown that will last forever.

1 CORINTHIANS 9:24−25

Never, never, never give up!
WINSTON CHURCHILL

TWO YEARS EARLIER...

Crash!

The violent sound of a metal trash can bouncing past my head ripped me from a dream-filled, exhausted slumber. I sat bolt upright, hitting my head on the bunk above mine. Everything was dark.

Where am I?

A chorus of booming voices erupted all around, shouting, "Get up! Move, move, MOVE!"

I rolled out of bed onto the floor. Confusion reigned. Things were falling as bunks and wall lockers were being toppled. Shouts echoed off wood floors and walls.

What time is it?

The lights blazed on. A chaotic scene assaulted me: men in shorts and T-shirts running in all directions, everyone yelling. The earsplitting sound of an M-60 machine gun ripped through the confined space of the old World War II—era barracks that had been quiet only seconds earlier. Even though the weapon was firing only blanks, the sound was deafening and chased away any vestiges of sleep that may have been lingering in my brain.

I checked my watch: 0200 hours.

Then I remembered what day it was.

Day one of the Ranger Indoctrination Program, also known as RIP.

I stumbled out of the barracks with the rest of the Ranger candidates, all of us survivors of thirteen weeks of infantry basic training, then three more weeks of Airborne school.

If we thought the last four months were grueling, the concept was about to be redefined for us.

When the Ranger recruiters had visited our battalion in basic training and given a briefing describing the Ranger regiment, more than four hundred men had indicated an interest in becoming a Ranger. A few of them never made it out of basic training or washed out during jump school. Of the one hundred and fifty or so men who had reported to RIP with this class, only about forty were part of that original group from basic—about one-tenth of those who initially gave it a shot.

Immediately after the Airborne graduation ceremony, several hard-looking RIP instructors, called tactical advisors/coordinators (TACs), were waiting there to collect us. They wore the distinctive uniform of the Airborne Ranger—starched, olive-drab jungle fatigues (the rest of the Army wore camouflage, so they really stood out), jungle boots, and the coveted black beret.

I had dreamed of wearing the black beret ever since high school, when a former Ranger taught my tenth grade Sunday school class. He had exuded a quiet confidence that whispered to me of mountains conquered and hard-fought battles won, and I wanted what he had. Nothing short of the Ranger beret would do.

As a matter of fact, I had decided not to purchase the maroon Airborne beret to wear at graduation, unlike most of my fellow soldiers, because I saw Airborne as a rung on the ladder, not a destination.

For me, it was the Rangers or nothing.

The day before, the TACs had ordered us to pick up our belongings and march (or stagger, in this case, underneath all our gear) the mile or so from the Airborne barracks to the RIP barracks, which sat atop "cardiac hill," a quarter mile of road rising two hundred near-vertical feet above the airfield. During the next three weeks we would become all too familiar with that hill.

The RIP barracks were actually a set of two-story clapboard buildings, unfinished bays on the inside with latrines at one end. Word had it they were the same barracks used by the original parachute test platoon in the 1940s. They were completely uninsulated, and from my bunk I could see through the cracks in the clapboard wall to "red square," a grassless lot of Georgia clay between the buildings that was used for daily formations.

RIP could be thought of as tryouts for the Ranger regiment. The sole purpose of the three-week course was to weed out those who wouldn't be able to handle the rigorous demands of life in a special operations unit. And this purpose it performed flawlessly.

Wall lockers were assigned and then detailed briefings ran until almost 2300. We then had a final formation in front of the barracks and were released to unpack our belongings and get some sleep before first call, announced for 0500 the next morning. Most of us had hurriedly unpacked and slid into our bunks around midnight—only two hours before the surprise "ballistic wake-up" that we were now experiencing.

We piled out of the barracks and into the night, some men still dressing as they ran. Soon we were formed up in front of the barracks. Then one of our TACs, Staff Sergeant Schott, emerged from the building. The lights illuminating the square backlit his big, powerful frame as he stalked over and began pacing in front of us. He smiled menacingly, looking for all the world like a professional wrestler stalking the ring. Then he bellowed, "The dying cockroach! Everyone, on your backs!"

IF GOD MEANT FOR ME TO BECOME A RANGER, THERE WOULD BE NO STOPPING ME.

As if dropped by the force of his voice alone, the entire company fell to the ground, though we were not exactly sure what the "dying cockroach" was. We were then instructed to lie flat on our backs with our hands and feet pointed skyward, heads off the ground, as the TACs waded around and through the formation, hurling curses and insults at us.

Staff Sergeant Schott stood in front of us, hands on hips. "Ladies," he boomed sarcastically, "here is where we find out how bad you want to be a Ranger. If you can't keep your arms and legs perpendicular to the ground and your head out of the dirt, you don't want it bad enough, and we don't need you. So go ahead and take a rest if you get tired. Just get up and go see Staff Sergeant Porter at the rear of the formation, and he will sign off on your orders to be reassigned for the needs of the Army."

The phrase *needs of the Army* struck fear in the hearts of the strongest men. This meant you would be sent to wherever the Army had the fewest volunteers, which was often some desolate backwater base far from anything exciting. It could also mean that you'd be reassigned to a regular Army infantry unit, which in our minds represented one of the lowest dregs of military society. One thing was certain, however: Any assignment would be easier than what we were currently experiencing.

Five minutes passed.

"Now," Staff Sergeant Schott continued, swaggering in front of the forest of trembling arms and legs, "we have to get rid of more than 60 percent of you girls in the next three weeks. So to make our job a little easier, we've decided to speed up the process a bit. With that in mind, you are going to remain in this position until fully half of you give up or collapse, whichever comes first. So get comfortable."

A collective groan rose from our ranks. That meant that more than seventy men must quit before we could get up. About thirty men quit immediately. *Good*, I thought, *almost halfway there.* Still, it amazed me that so many had come this far only to quit as soon as it got difficult.

I would never have been able to take this if I didn't believe there was a purpose behind it. That lesson had been driven home a couple of months earlier in basic training. We were there to become soldiers, plain and simple. The hardship that we endured now would leave us better prepared for the life-or-death struggle that might come later. If this had been some kind of summer camp, none of us would have stayed past the first day. Simply understanding that the misery we were being put through was to prepare us for battle made it more bearable.

I once heard a youth minister talk about the confidence that comes with knowing that everything happens for a reason. The belief that my life wasn't a random journey, but that I was created for a specific mission, meant that God wasn't going to leave me hanging. If He meant for me to become a Ranger, there would be no stopping me. This conviction gave me peace, and I drew on some of that peace now.

All my life I'd wondered how I would hold up in a situation like this, an all-out battle of endurance. I had imagined being locked in this kind of struggle, teeth clenched, determined to be the last man standing. Only in this case, I wasn't standing. I was on my back in the red Georgia clay with all my extremities pointing straight up in the air. And the exertion of it was already making me start to quiver.

Ten minutes.

Our RIP instructors paced around the formation, watching, waiting for someone to let his head touch the ground or bend his knees to rest. They berated us with mocking, jeering remarks. They tried to trick us into thinking that they weren't looking—a few guys fell for it and let their heads touch earth for a few precious seconds of rest. Gone. When the TACs caught someone slacking, they immediately descended on him like lions on their prey, dragging him roughly out of the formation, consigned to the "needs of the Army."

A lot was at stake here. I thought about how my life would change if I gave up now. They would probably send me to the frozen tundra of Alaska, which is where I was slated to go before I volunteered for the Rangers. I really don't like to be cold. More than that, Alaska seemed about as far as one could get from any excitement that the Army had to offer.

Fifteen minutes.

More men quit. The pain in my abdominal muscles was excruciating. I gulped in short, deliberate breaths, gasping for air to feed oxygen-starved muscles. The cold, humid morning penetrated my now-bloodless arms and legs.

I had made myself a promise on the day that I raised my right hand and took the oath of enlistment. Not knowing what trials awaited me in the next four years, my biggest fear was not being tough enough, not measuring up. I didn't think I could live with myself if I failed. So I resolved never to quit, never to fall out. I would make it or die trying. At barely eighteen, my fledgling manhood was on the line.

Right now, however, I could feel my resolve beginning to waver, and it scared me.

In Airborne school, you often heard the statement, "They can make it harder, but they can't make it longer!" We fell back on this when it seemed the instructors were piling it on just for fun, making us wait to get into the chow hall, or ordering extra practice falls. After all, at the end of three weeks, they had to let us out, one way or another. There hadn't been a single time in Airborne school when I had doubted I would make it. As long as I wasn't killed or injured on a jump, Airborne school was a done deal.

But this... this was different.

I knew they couldn't leave us in this position forever, but I was *equally* unsure that I could outlast the roughly twenty or so men who would have to quit before we could move on to the next ordeal. I had no intention of quitting, but I didn't know how long my body would hold out. The mental anguish of that prospect was almost more painful than the physical torture of the dying cockroach. Almost.

Twenty minutes.

I closed my eyes and tried to forget the intense pain in the muscles of my neck and abs. My hands and feet were numb from lack of blood and the cold, but the rest of my body was drenched in the sweat of exertion.

I thought back to a conversation with my mother as I was leaving for basic training. "I only want to know what you had for breakfast, Son," she had said with a pained smile. She was always worried about the difficulties I'd be facing on active duty. To her it was simply easier not to know. "I know that if this is in God's plan for you, you will be safe. But just remember what your grandmother always says, 'Thou shall not tempt the Lord thy God.'"

I grinned imperceptibly at the memory. Strangely enough, I *did* feel like this was where I was supposed to be. Why God wanted me here wasn't entirely clear to me at present. I had mused in my journal that perhaps He needed a hit man. More likely, I figured, the skills I was learning in the Army would be used in some far-flung mission field. Maybe He would call me to smuggle Bibles or undertake some other dangerous adventure for His purposes. Sounded like fun to me.

How did I *know* that God wanted me here? Since I was in the sixth grade, joining the military had been a passion. Our pastor had once said something that hit me like a stun gun: "God doesn't contradict Himself. If He wants you to go to Africa, then you won't find peace doing anything else. He will put a passion in you that corresponds with the plan that He has for you." The way I saw things, finding God's will for my life was simply a matter of pursuing the things that made me passionate, then looking for God to open and close doors along the way. So far, this plan seemed to be working.

In high school, I had liked photography and journalism and enjoyed some measure of success at it. I often took pictures at high school football games and sold them to the local newspaper. It was a great experience, and I entertained thoughts of becoming a professional photographer. But try as I might, nothing seemed to work out when I pursued that vocation. When I checked into the Army, however, everything fell into place.

Hey, I can take a hint.

Growing up, I knew several World War II vets from my church. I hung on their every word as they recounted stories of combat in occupied France and around the world. These stories made me long for a more dangerous existence. Life in my hometown of Carson City, Nevada, was too sedate for my taste. Surrounded by a loving, functional family and involved in a caring church full of godly men and women—it was all too safe. And dull.

I felt a sort of warm smile inside as I remembered being twelve, hiking in the mountains behind my house after school, just wishing some kind of catastrophe would happen to liven things up. A tornado, a brush fire, or a landslide would have been great—anything to break the monotony of life in a small town.

The dying cockroach, however, wasn't exactly what I had in mind.

Thirty minutes.

I tried to count the number of men that were left, but I was in such agony that my mind couldn't focus on the task long enough to complete it. As best I could tell, about fifteen men needed to quit before this ordeal would be finished. Actually, fifteen men had to quit before we could even get *started*. It wasn't yet three in the morning—for all intents and purposes, RIP hadn't even begun. I wondered what awaited those who passed this first test. Rest? Doubtful.

I had to make a conscious effort to keep breathing. It took everything I had to keep from simply collapsing. The frozen tundra of Alaska was starting to look better, almost bearable.

I looked to the left, and my gaze locked with that of the man next to me. He was shaking uncontrollably and had tears in his eyes. I could tell that he wanted desperately not to quit; but gravity was winning the battle, and his arms and legs slowly sank to the ground. Even though his failure meant one fewer man for me to compete with, my heart went out to him. I hadn't even had a chance to learn his name. Now I never would.

The TAC came over, and I could tell that he saw the defeat in the man's eyes. "Come on, son," he said quietly. "You're done here." I turned away as the soldier let out a sob, the pitiful sound of a man broken.

Forty minutes.

A few more quit. They got up and joined the dejected ranks of men behind our formation, standing at parade rest and not daring to talk or move, lest they suffer the wrath of the RIP instructors. We were down to those who really wanted it badly, and I wondered how long this could go on, even though we had to lose only a couple more before it would be over.

Some of the dropouts surprised me. They had been the biggest, most athletic-looking in the bunch. I had seen them in the barracks the night before, muscles bulging as they strutted around the communal bathroom. Intimidating. At only five feet nine and less than one hundred and thirty pounds, I had wondered how I'd ever be able to compete with them. But this challenge was more about mental determination than physical stamina.

I thought again about what I was doing here. *Why am I so driven to pursue this? What does God have in store?* The weekend before we graduated from Airborne school, I had attended a local church. A man named David Randol had been my Sunday school teacher in Texas my junior year. He had bright red hair, and everyone, including his wife, called him Rooster. He and his family had recently moved to Columbus, Georgia, so Rooster could take a job as youth pastor. I don't believe in coincidence, and it was clear to me that one of the reasons God had sent him here was to provide me with a church home with some familiar faces. To get away from the Army, even for a day, and feel like a civilian again was just what I needed to stay sane.

The last Sunday school lesson had been from the book of Proverbs. "He holds victory in store for the upright" was about all I could remember from it. That verse had been pasted in my memory for the past week. It struck me now as a cruel irony that, at the moment, I wasn't upright but flat on my back. While I was sure that by "upright" the verse really meant something like "blameless," that didn't make me feel much better.

I knew there were plenty of areas in my life that needed attention. But I really was trying to follow what I believed to be God's will. I hoped that would be good enough. Then it hit me: God is more concerned with who I am *becoming* than with what I am *doing*— He would undoubtedly use this experience to shape me into someone more closely resembling His Son. This wasn't just Army training; it was *life* training. I clung to the hope that He wouldn't allow me to fail at either one.

Forty-five minutes.

I was so numb by this point that it was almost like the pain was happening to someone else. Almost.

If I had known during the first ten minutes of this that we were going to be here this long, I probably would have quit then. Now, however, I felt a surge of energy as I craned my neck to catch a glimpse of the formation of quitters behind us. I had outlasted more than sixty-five men, and I certainly wasn't going to be the last one to quit—not when victory was so close.

Then one more man dropped his arms and legs to the ground, and Staff Sergeant Schott's thunderous voice boomed, "That's it, men. On your feet!"

Just like that, it was over.

With a collective groan of relief, we all rolled over and dragged ourselves to our knees. Some of us wobbled a bit the first time we tried to rise on bloodless legs, but we were steadied by the man to our left or right. As we helped each other to stand, those of us who had made it could already feel the beginnings of a brotherly bond that would only grow stronger with each new trial we faced together over the next fifteen days.

"Company, atten-SHUN!"

We locked into formation, arms by our sides, eyes straight ahead. Though still a bit unstable, we did our best to stand perfectly still, fearful of doing anything to set off the TACs.

"You have exactly two minutes to get your rucksack and load-bearing equipment and be back here with your boots on. FALL OUT!"

The formation evaporated as we quickly funneled into the barracks through its one small door. Two minutes later we were headed down the road in formation at a full run to our first experience with something that we were to become very familiar with—the Downing Mile obstacle course.

Day one had begun.

THE ARMY VS. GOD

Everything that I am or ever will be is either God's intention or my mistake.
CHUCK HOLTON, AGE 15, JOURNAL ENTRY

Many are the plans in a man's heart,
but it is the LORD's purpose that prevails.
PROVERBS 19:21

Twelve grueling nonstop days later, our numbers had thinned even further. Endless road marches, skills tests, and discipline exercises had pared the class from one hundred and fifty men to only forty-two.

The last two weeks had been a blur of physical and mental challenges that had pushed to the limits of our endurance and beyond. After the first few days I was unwillingly named class leader and forced to take on the additional responsibility of keeping track of everyone and their specific duties. Whenever someone fouled up, I shared the blame. I had done the same job in basic training for all but the first three weeks and was not happy with being "volunteered" by the TACs to shoulder the task again here. The job did have one privilege, however: I was exempt from the nightly fireguard duty that everyone else had to pull at least twice a week.

The benefit was overrated, though, since I was usually up before everyone else anyway, getting schedules ready for the day ahead. I decided that God had an ironic sense of humor, putting me in that role, since the gift of organization seemed to flee from me like feathers before the wind.

On Sunday we were given a pass for a few hours. I was in an especially good mood, having just convinced the TACs that some-one else needed experience as class leader, so they had replaced me. In addition, Thanksgiving was fast approaching, and we were all looking forward to two weeks of leave after graduation the follow-ing Wednesday. For most of us, it had been an uninterrupted twenty weeks of training since the first day of basic. To say that we were ready for a break would have been a waste of words.

My good friend Mike Hare had driven out from Texas to attend my graduation. He was also a friend of Rooster and Anita's, and so when my RIP class was granted seven hours off, Mike took me to Rooster's house for some *real* food and a little relaxation. Mike and I discussed our plans to drive back to Texas as soon as RIP was over and I was put on leave. I could hardly wait to see my family.

Mike checked his watch and said, "We'd better be getting back. What time is your formation?"

"Uh, 1630," I said, stretching as I got up from Rooster's living room floor. "I guess you're right. It's only three-thirty, but it wouldn't hurt to get back a little early." We grabbed our jackets and said our good-byes to Rooster and Anita. Then we jumped into

Mike's Toyota for the half-hour drive back to Fort Benning.

When we drove up to the RIP barracks, it was one minute until four. As we drove up, I could tell immediately that something was wrong. The place looked deserted. Why weren't men going in and out of the barracks getting ready for formation? When we drove past the barracks, what I saw on the other side made my blood run cold.

The entire company was already in uniform, standing at attention.

Breathing suddenly became a conscious act as I realized that the formation must have been at 1600, not 1630 as I had thought.

"This is bad, Mike. I've gotta go. I'll call you later."

I bounded out of the car before it even came to a stop and started to run toward the formation, when I realized that I was still in civilian clothes. I couldn't go like that. I turned and darted into the barracks.

I was still feverishly pulling on my uniform when men started coming back into the barracks. The formation was over. I was mortified. If you wanted to get kicked out of RIP, being late for a formation would do it. *Missing* one left no doubt.

One of my classmates came over, wearing a grave look. "Sergeant Schott wants to see you immediately."

Shock set in as the room began to blur in front of me. My mouth suddenly wouldn't work right, and a feeble "OK" was all I could muster.

Staff Sergeant Schott was standing outside the TAC office. I ran up to him and locked up at parade rest. "Private Holton reporting!" I stood before him awaiting the explosion.

Staff Sergeant Schott didn't yell at me, however. That made it even worse.

"Well, Holton, three days from graduation, and you had to

blow it. Staff Sergeant Porter will decide tomorrow if you will re-cycle to the next RIP class or leave for good. You might as well start getting packed. I'll call for you tomorrow. Now move out."

"Sergeant, I…"

"MOVE OUT!" he thundered.

I ran back to the barracks, barely able to breathe. I wished I could crawl in a hole and disappear. Instead, I walked dejectedly into the barracks, where everyone was getting ready to go to chow. I tried to avoid their stares. A buddy named Floyd Coke stopped by my bunk and asked, "What'd he say?"

Rummaging around with my head in my locker, hoping to avoid a conversation, I answered, "He said he'd call for me tomor-row." My eyes were starting to water. Coke, one of the men who had been in my platoon since basic training, turned away, emitting a low whistle through clenched teeth.

I coasted through dinner on automatic pilot, not caring what was on my plate, unable even to think. Then we were given free time until lights-out at 2200. I sat on my lower bunk, pulled out my worn black leather journal, and started writing. It was something I'd done since junior high school whenever life didn't make sense. Recording my thoughts at times like these usually helped me to make sense of them, as I hoped it would now.

SUNDAY, 22 NOVEMBER 1987

I'm supposed to graduate from RIP in three days. I've just spent two of the toughest weeks of my life here. I really blew it today. We had a pass this weekend, and Mike is here, so he and I were at Rooster's house. I got back this afternoon a little bit late. Boy, what a bad move. Now, I'm facing the possibility of having to spend another month here as a recycle or being kicked out altogether. This is my absolute worst nightmare. I believe that God is stronger than the Army and can influence my TACs into allowing me to stay. The question is, does He WANT to?

Oh, you can't imagine the sincerity of my prayers.

I have to trust in the Lord and cling to that trust with all the hope I can muster. It's like I'm putting my life down as a bet between God and the Army. I really hope I don't lose the bet. Getting recycled would seriously scramble my life at this point, to say nothing of being kicked out altogether. All the plans I have made, and that others have made on my behalf, would be shot. I'd have to face everyone with the fact that I had failed. And my witness would receive a serious tarnish, because I have been saying to people all along that I believe God didn't let me come all this way to fail. Just this morning I was telling one of the guys here that I think I am where God wants me to be because everything keeps falling right into place in my life. I would look like a real fool to all the guys that I've shared God with around here, because as they graduated, they'd be saying, "I wonder what happened to the God he was so sure would get him through."

I'm scared. That's all there is to it. Please quiet my fear, Lord, and please don't let me down.

After lights-out that night, I lay awake in my bunk, praying. Over the preceding months my prayer life had suffered. I was always so exhausted that I'd normally be asleep ten seconds after crawling between the cold, starched sheets of my rack. But not tonight. I was tired, sure, but my future was now in jeopardy because of a needless mistake, and the blame rested squarely on the man in my bunk.

Airborne school had taught me a great lesson in the meaning of faith. Simply having an interest in becoming an Airborne trooper might have coaxed me into putting on a harness. Curiosity might have prodded me onto the plane and even given me the nerve to peer out of the open jump door in flight. None of those actions, however, would have gotten me Airborne-qualified. To earn that classification required stepping out the door, putting my knees in the breeze, and trusting my life to the skill of an unknown, overworked parachute rigger and about nine hundred and fifty square feet of parachute nylon.

There's a line where the floor of the aircraft meets the open jump door. That line is where curiosity stops and commitment begins. Someone who is merely interested in parachuting would never cross that line.

I had known people who were "interested" Christians as well. They attended church every week, and some even sang in the choir or held prominent positions. But for them, being a Christian was really more of an academic pursuit than a relationship with God built on trust. When it came to giving God control over their relationships, their children, or their pocketbooks, it was easier for them to lean on their own abilities than to surrender to His. I had shown up in that category myself from time to time.

Surrender. That's really what it's about, isn't it? Airborne school had taught me that whether it was jumping out of a perfectly good airplane at thirteen hundred feet or letting go of my need to be in control of my life, the act of surrendering was the same.

And now it was time to surrender to His will yet again.

Here I was asking God to pull my chestnuts out of the fire, when it was my own carelessness that had put them there. I realized that I couldn't blame God if I got kicked out. He didn't put me in this situation. I had done it to myself and could think of no reason why I deserved to be saved from my own stupidity.

Then it hit me. Did I ever *deserve* to be saved? This wasn't the first time I had been in a mess because of my own bad choices. God had come to the rescue before. A verse from the Bible came to mind: "I will never leave you nor forsake you." I couldn't remember the chapter and verse, but I was glad that at least that fragment was still in my memory bank. All that memorization in Sunday school as a kid was paying off. I figured out later that this promise was found in Deuteronomy 31:6.

> "Be strong and courageous. Do not be afraid or terrified
> because of them, for the LORD your God goes with you;
> he will never leave you nor forsake you."

Slowly, the sense of peace I'd felt the first day after the ballistic wake-up began to wash over me again. In that moment, I *knew* God hadn't forgotten about me. He still had a plan for my life, and it would be accomplished one way or another—in spite of myself. If I was meant to be a Ranger, not even my own mistakes could stop me, as long as I did my best and put the outcome in His capable hands.

I rolled over and went to sleep.

The next morning after PT, I didn't wait to be called to the TAC office. I went to the door and knocked. It was something that a student just didn't do, but I figured there wasn't much more to lose at this point.

"What are you doing here?" Sergeant Schott barked. A gorilla-like chest strained the buttons on his starched green uniform as he set down a monstrous coffee mug with a scowl.

"I need to speak with you, Sergeant." I stood stiffly at parade rest.

Staff Sergeant Porter was there, too, sitting on the edge of the desk. They sat and looked at me for a minute, then exchanged glances. "Get in here, Holton," Porter said icily.

I complied.

"What do you have to say?" Staff Sergeant Schott said, his tone less aggressive than before.

"I DON'T BELIEVE THAT GOD PUT ME HERE TO FAIL."

"Sergeant, I just want to ask you to consider allowing me to graduate with the class and not recycle me. I take full responsibility for my actions yesterday and admit that I was careless, and it should not have happened. However, I'd like to point out that until yesterday afternoon I have had a perfect record here, with not a single minus to my name for the entire course. I believe I performed well as class leader and would just like to ask that you take this into account before you make the decision to recycle me. In addition..." My voice faltered for a moment.

Both TACs were staring at me like they couldn't believe what they were hearing. "Is there something else?" Staff Sergeant Porter asked, seeing that I hadn't quite finished.

"Yes, Sergeant. I don't believe that God put me here to fail."

"What?" Their eyebrows shot up in unison. Staff Sergeant

Schott almost choked on his coffee.

"Sergeant," I continued, hoping that my voice sounded more confident than I felt, "I've done well at every level since I joined the Army in July. I don't think it's been that way for no reason. I believe that God put me here for a purpose, and I simply can't believe that I've gotten this close only to fail because of my own stupid mistake."

Both men were silent, their faces unreadable.

I continued. "I will gladly pay for my error. I'll do anything you say. Just please don't kick me out."

The TACs looked at each other again. Then Staff Sergeant Porter turned and looked out the small window behind him for a moment. He said in a low voice, "Go to chow. I'll call you in afterward and let you know what we've decided."

"Roger, Sergeant." I did an about-face and left.

I have never prayed more over a single meal before or since. After breakfast, we had about a half hour before the buses came to take us to the field for our final patrol. I was mopping the communal bathroom when a private came in.

"Staff Sergeant Porter wants to see you right away," he said.

Did they ever want to see you any other way? In four months of Army training, I had never been told, "The drill sergeant wants to see you in half an hour."

I double-timed it to the TAC office. My stomach was in knots.

Staff Sergeant Porter was there alone, standing beside the desk piled high with papers. "Take a seat," he said.

The sinking feeling in my gut helped pull me down to the chair. He would never tell me to sit unless he was about to break some bad news to me.

He pulled up a chair across from me and sat looking at me for a moment. I waited for the hammer to fall. The short silence was crushing. Was this it? My eyes froze on a spot behind Staff Sergeant Porter's head; I was unable to focus or even blink.

Then he said, "I've decided to let you stay."

I almost threw up on him.

Then he continued. "But you are going to *wish* you had been recycled."

I didn't know what to say to that. What could be worse than having to endure the dying cockroach a second time? I kept quiet and simply nodded.

"You are to report to the charge of quarters and sign in with him every thirty minutes from lights out at 2200 to first call at 0445 for the remainder of your time here. If you miss even one sign-in, you might as well pack up and leave. In addition, if you so much as sneeze out of turn between now and graduation, you'll be out of here so fast it will make your head spin. Is that clear?"

I stood up. "Roger, Sergeant. Thank you."

"You won't thank me by Wednesday. Now get out of here."

"Hooah, Sergeant." I turned and practically sprinted out of the room.

God had come through. It was a sad testament to the level of my faith that I was so surprised. The lightness that suddenly invaded my spirit made me feel like I could positively float.

God saved me in spite of my mistakes, but I still had to suffer the consequences. Over the next forty-eight hours, as I went two nights with no more than twenty minutes' sleep at a stretch, I realized something else: Now there was no way that I'd be able to take credit for becoming a Ranger if I made it—it was all God's doing. I'd heard at church that God shares His glory with no one, and He was making that fact abundantly clear to me.

On Wednesday morning, my friend Mike was there to watch as our class participated in a short, understated graduation ceremony. We all wore dress uniforms, unadorned except for our marksmanship badges and shiny new jump wings.

The moment that we put on our new black berets for the first time signified more for me than just a rite of passage into an elite group of warriors. Somehow that round felt hat meant much more. It was a symbol of my journey into manhood, in a spiritual sense as much as a physical one.

But the journey had just begun.

3

SOLDIER TO
SERVANT

Endure hardship with us like a good soldier of Christ Jesus.

2 TIMOTHY 2:3

Sweat saves blood.

GENERAL ERWIN ROMMEL

MONDAY, 8 FEBRUARY 1988, 0340 HOURS

The silence was so intense that I could hear it, a soft ringing in my
ears that was only there when all was completely still.

It was the worst time of night, the time when boredom pressed
in as if in competition with the exhaustion that was trying to force
me to sleep. I had tried every means of staying alert that I could
think of—jumping jacks, deep knee bends, running in place. I had
done more than three hundred push-ups to keep the blood pump-
ing, but I was afraid that if I tried to do more I'd fall asleep on my
face. A radio would have been helpful, but one wasn't allowed. I had
read until my eyes had gone blurry. I had caught up on my journal

and written letters until my hand started wandering off the page.

The Army isn't all excitement and adventure.

As a matter of fact, so far this job had involved far more tedium than I had expected. I don't know what made me think I was in for nonstop thrills, but I had been wrong.

I had to stay awake. I had less than four hours until the end of my twenty-four-hour shift as charge of quarters, or CQ. This was a duty that fell to each man in the platoon about once every other month. One private and one noncommissioned officer were charged with sitting by the phone at the front door of the barracks. Their duties included taking messages, signing in visitors, cleaning the offices at night, and basically keeping a lid on things until the next two men came at 0730 to take their place. The only good thing about it was that you got the next day off to sleep.

My squad leader, Staff Sergeant Friar, was sharing the duty with me tonight, but he had left me in charge of the telephone while he made the rounds of the company area.

God help the man who fell asleep on CQ. Something like that would mean a quick trip "down the road" to the 197th Infantry Regiment, a low-speed "leg" unit, our derogatory term for any non-airborne group. That might not be actual hell for a Ranger, but it was awfully close. The fact that the Ranger regiment was an all-volunteer unit meant that you could be kicked out at any time for not maintaining the unit's ultrahigh standards. Men had been let go for things such as falling out of a road march. At any rate, I had worked too hard to get here to throw it away for something as simple as staying awake. Only it wasn't as simple as I had hoped it would be.

The door to the dayroom slammed shut. I was jerked out of my reverie to see Staff Sergeant Friar walking toward me.

"You'd better get up, Holton, or the drone monster is gonna get you."

"Roger, Sergeant." I was already on my feet. I couldn't decide if Staff Sergeant Friar liked me or not. Either way, I wanted to make a good impression. "Should I go check out the company area?"

"I just did, but you might as well check it again. It's harder to fall asleep walking than it is sitting."

"Hooah, Sergeant." *Hooah* was the quintessential Ranger answer for everything. Depending on the context, it could mean almost anything, but in this case, it was like saying, "I'm on it!"

I stepped out the door into the cold pre-dawn. In Georgia, it didn't get cold often; but when it did, the dampness drilled it right through you. I surveyed the battalion area and wiggled my toes inside my jungle boots.

My toes were still numb from the three-day training mission we had just completed. The doctor said they might be that way for quite some time and warned me to take better care of my feet or risk permanent damage.

It had been my first big training exercise. I was assigned to carry a Squad Automatic Weapon, nicknamed the SAW. A smaller version of the M-60 machine gun, it uses the same type of 5.56 mm ammunition as the ubiquitous M-16 rifle. However, the SAW fires more than seven hundred rounds per minute and weighs about twenty-one pounds with a full two-hundred-round box of ammo. Quite a bit more cumbersome than the M-16, the SAW took some getting used to.

Our platoon had been flown into a small clearing in the northern reaches of Fort Benning's vast training area. We had "fast-roped" in, another first for me. I had seen people rappel from helicopters, but this was different and, at the time, still classified. The Black Hawk helicopter would hover over the insertion area and drop a long polypropylene rope, about as thick as my wrist, connected to a boom above the door. Wearing thick leather gloves, we would then grab the rope and slide down as if it were a fireman's pole. The trick was to get to the bottom as quickly as possible without breaking any bones or equipment when you landed. Once you hit the ground, you needed to roll out of the way or else you'd end up underneath a large pile of Rangers and their gear.

We practiced fast-roping from a tower in our training area before the mission, and it had been a piece of cake—just the kind of thing I had joined the Army to do. When it came to exiting the helicopter, however, I made one slight error: I missed the rope.

Not completely, though. I just overshot it with my hands and ended up hugging it with my arms and legs all the way down. While that provided just enough braking power to keep me from being seriously injured, it didn't keep me from running into my team leader, Specialist Hill. Three-quarters of the way down, I knocked him off the rope ten feet above the ground, and then I fell and landed on him. The force of the impact broke the ballistic nylon sling that held the SAW on my back. It wasn't exactly the kind of impression that I had hoped to make on Specialist Hill. Fortunately, neither of us was seriously hurt, though Hill may have contemplated hurting me at that point.

Once our platoon had assembled at the edge of the clearing, we quickly moved into the woods to a *hide site* several kilometers away. We set up a patrol base, which is basically a triangular perimeter, each squad taking one leg of the triangle, with machine guns manning each corner. Our platoon sergeant, Sergeant First Class Kelly, instructed us to dig fighting positions. We took turns scraping out shallow holes to lie in and then settled in to wait for darkness to fall.

Hours passed. We were spread about ten feet apart around the perimeter, too far to talk without giving away our position. I had no idea what was going on. No one had bothered to tell me how long we would be here. All I knew was that I was bored, hungry, and painfully cold.

Our unit's standard operating procedure specified that we were not allowed to wear a coat or anything that would put us "out of uniform." So in order to stay warm, everyone wore thick polypropylene long underwear under their uniforms. We called it "hot gear."

It was almost completely dark when I felt a hand on my shoulder. "Let's move," Specialist Hill whispered. He turned and melted into the darkness. I got up quickly and struggled for a moment with my pack and weapon. A gloved hand grabbed me and propelled me forward. "Move it, newbie!" I could hear the annoyance in my team leader's voice. Everyone was waiting for me. I had a lot to learn about being ready to move at any time.

We moved out in single file, keeping about three meters apart in the black moonless night. Every man had little glow-in-the-dark patches sewn on the back of his rucksack to make it easier for the guy following. Without lights of any kind, we traveled cross-country as quietly as possible. It took about twenty minutes before my feet started to thaw out, but by that time my large rucksack was starting to feel more like two.

By 2200 we were getting close to our objective. The platoon stopped and we all took a knee, each man facing alternately left or right, pulling security. We stayed there for over an hour in complete silence while our leaders did a reconnaissance of the objective. The frigid night air slowly turned the sweat on my uniform to ice water. It felt like someone had put a large rock into my rucksack. I wanted to flop down on my back and rest, but no one else was doing it, and I certainly wasn't going to be the first. We had to "stay tactical."

By the time the lieutenant and platoon sergeant returned, we were all shivering and I felt an inch shorter. Once again, I had no idea what was going on. My knees were killing me.

Sergeant Friar came around and gave us whispered instructions. Our objective was less than five hundred meters to our front. We were to be the assault team. The weapons squad would set up a support position and begin firing on the objective. We would then bound across the objective by teams, covering each other as we went. Once the area was secure, we would retrace our steps back here, get our rucksacks, and link up with the rest of the platoon.

Specialist Hill saw the confused look on my face. "Do exactly what I do and you'll be fine."

I nodded. I could do that. I honestly didn't understand most of what Sergeant Friar had said, but I trusted Specialist Hill to get me there and back in one piece. And there was one fact I did grasp—I would finally get to put down my humongous pack, if only for a while. I nearly floated without its debilitating weight as I followed behind Specialist Hill toward the objective.

The raid went well. Our platoon cleared the objective of "enemy," which were other Rangers assigned to be opposing forces for this mission. However, as we bounded across the objective, I seemed to be moving slower than everyone else. My team leader kept yelling at me to get moving. Although I did my best to follow Specialist Hill, I felt like I was stuck in a dream, moving in slow motion while everyone else was in real time. I hoped that with experience I'd get better, but I secretly feared that there was something wrong with me. Why couldn't I move faster?

Once the raid was successfully completed, we retraced our route quickly and quietly back to the rucksacks; then we headed to the hide site via a different route. Trudging along in single file through the thick Georgia pines, exhaustion started to catch up with me. I felt like a dead man walking.

The signal for a "danger area" came down through the patrol. It was a river crossing—actually a creek, knee-deep and maybe twenty yards across. We posted security in each direction and started sending Rangers across one at a time. When it was my turn, I was instantly restored to alertness by the bracing temperature of the water. Once on the far side, I was eager to get moving again before my feet had a chance to freeze solid. My guess was that the temperature was hovering in the midthirties.

An hour later, my jungle boots still weren't dry as we quietly moved back into the hide site. I found the hole I had dug earlier and dropped my ruck in front of it.

Specialist Hill came over. "Get in your hole and change your socks. Then pull security while I do the same."

"Hooah, Specialist." It wasn't lost on me that he was allowing me to change first, and in a small way, it began to register that leadership isn't as much about asserting one's authority as it is about putting the needs of your men before your own. I had noticed how all the officers in our unit always ate last. It was more of a respected tradition than a standard operating procedure. As a child, I had memorized Luke 22:26: "But among you, those who are the greatest should take the lowest rank, and the leader should be like

> TRUE LEADERSHIP MEANS PUTTING THE NEEDS OF YOUR MEN BEFORE YOUR OWN.

a servant" (NLT). Lately this verse was taking on new and deeper meaning for me.

I sat down in the shallow fighting position and quickly pulled off my boots. I massaged my frozen toes for a moment before slipping them into a dry pair of socks. I may as well have been rubbing ice cubes. Besides, the dry socks went back into my still-wet boots. I laced up, grabbed my weapon, and turned over to lie prone, facing away from the perimeter. I waved at Specialist Hill, who took his turn changing his socks.

We hadn't eaten anything since the mission had begun nearly eighteen hours earlier. It was now about three in the morning, and I felt like I could have eaten my old pair of socks. Had they forgotten to feed us?

I lay there in the dark feeling like a soggy sugar cookie and wishing that I knew what was going on. Pursuing God's purpose for your life is often like that. Sometimes I'm privy to so little of God's plan that my part in it is nothing short of bewildering. But as I'm a grunt in God's army, it's not my job to question His motives, only to trust Him and execute the orders that I'm given.

I snatched an hour or so of fitful sleep between pulling guard duty and trying to keep from freezing. Just before morning twilight, Specialist Hill woke me up for "stand to." During the French and Indian War, the natives would often attack just before dawn, so the Army began the practice of stand to, where everyone was awake and pulling security for the last half hour before sunrise. Apparently this was very successful, so the Army has continued the practice to the present day.

The French and Indians haven't attacked since.

I lay in the hole behind my rucksack, which was camouflaged with leaves and a small piece of netting. Soon my feet started to lose the struggle to keep warm—the temperature had dropped to around twenty-eight degrees, and no amount of wiggling my toes or kicking the sides of the hole worked any longer. I could feel the penetrating cold crawling steadily from my toes and up my feet. It was an excruciating sensation, and I gritted my teeth to keep from crying out. I wondered if this was what frostbite felt like, but I didn't want to say anything about it. I knew that everyone else had to be just as cold.

I wanted desperately to tough this out, to suffer my share of hardship, but I had never before experienced this kind of intense, relentless pain. My face contorted in agony, and a tear escaped and traveled down my nose, mingling with the camouflage paint and grime on my face. I was glad that no one else could see me grimacing.

After a while, Staff Sergeant Friar came around checking on our squad. He reached my hole and tapped me on the leg. "You doing OK?"

"Hooah, Sergeant."

"How's your feet?"

"Real cold."

"Mine, too." He looked at me for a moment. "They are bringing in a medevac helicopter for a couple of guys who are complaining of frostbite." His unspoken question lingered in the frozen air.

"I'm all right, Sergeant," I grunted. As much as I would have liked to catch that helicopter to someplace warm, I couldn't stand the thought of leaving everyone else out here—it would have been too much like quitting.

"I'd better make sure. Take your boots off."

"Roger, Sergeant." I sat up and quickly removed my boots and socks. My feet were raw, and the skin had a cold, waxy look like that of a cadaver.

Staff Sergeant Friar pinched my big toe. "Hmmm. Looks like frost nip, at least. We'd better get those taken care of quick. Are you sure you don't want to catch that medevac?"

This was my chance. Not to get warm, but to show Staff Sergeant Friar that I could tough it out. "Negative, Sergeant."

He waved Specialist Hill over to my position. "You've got to get Holton squared away, or he's going to lose his toes."

Specialist Hill scowled. "Roger, Sergeant." He didn't hesitate. Unbuckling his web belt and pulling up his BDU top, hot gear, and brown Army T-shirt, he grabbed my feet and placed them directly against his abdomen. He let loose a string of muttered curses through clenched teeth as my frozen feet immediately sucked the heat out of his body. The look on his face clearly indicated that I wasn't his favorite person at that moment.

Staff Sergeant Friar moved on to check the rest of the squad, while I continued to warm my feet on Specialist Hill's abdomen. I sat there in agony as the blood started to creep back into my capillaries. I felt like I should say something, but I didn't know what. Specialist Hill was a no-nonsense soldier who never said much. When I could stand the silence no longer, I said, "I'm sorry, Specialist."

"Shut up, Holton," he said gruffly. "At least you didn't wimp out and take the medevac."

I looked to my left and caught the eye of another man in my squad. He was in his fighting position, pulling security; he grinned and gave me a thumbs-up.

I suddenly felt like I had done something right. I was moved by Specialist Hill's unflinching willingness to share my misery. As a newbie, I was really more of a liability out here than an asset, yet it seemed to mean something to these guys that I had chosen to stay. I longed to become a useful part of the team and gain the acceptance of these men. I was just beginning to understand that this wouldn't be accomplished through feats of daring or a quick wit, but through simply enduring hardship together.

Shared experience was the raw material out of which would be fashioned our esprit de corps. I realized that being a Ranger wasn't about getting through RIP and earning the right to wear a funny little black hat.

That was simply the price of admission.

Two nights later we completed our last mission of the exercise, a raid on a mock-enemy outpost. We took up positions around the objective area and waited for the three Black Hawk helicopters to swoop into our perimeter to pick us up. I watched through my goggles, amazed at the skill of the pilots as they hovered just a few feet above where I lay, the rotor wash kicking up a sandstorm. Static electricity caused the rotor blades to phosphoresce as the choppers landed.

After we piled into the helicopters for the short trip back to our barracks, I replayed the operation in my mind. We'd had about five hours of sleep in three days and eaten two meals during the entire field problem. The experience had taught me something important about myself: I was capable of enduring much more than I had ever imagined. I had fought off boredom, cold, pain, exhaustion, and hunger for the entire mission. And I felt like I had accomplished something.

But what had made the whole thing bearable was the knowledge that we were all in it together. I still needed to work on a few things, but I felt like I was becoming part of the team, part of something important—something larger than myself. My skills and endurance were being refined for something bigger.

No matter what else I might think about the difficulties I'd been facing in my training, I knew they were forging character and self-discipline—traits I hoped God would put to good use in my life. In those rare moments when I had leisure to reflect, I mused about the irony of making one's life harder in order to make it better. Running around from one party to another, as I sometimes did in high school, was beginning to seem like a cheap imitation of life compared to the full, purposeful life I was now experiencing.

> MY SKILLS AND
> ENDURANCE WERE
> BEING REFINED
> FOR SOMETHING
> BIGGER.

As a boy, I never would have guessed that happiness might be found on the path of greatest resistance. But then, the Bible is full of such incredible statements. Like the verse in Luke that says, "If you try to keep your life for yourself, you will lose it. But if you give up your life for me, you will find true life" (Luke 9:24, NLT). Over the last few months this verse had come alive for me as I learned that there is value in taking the hard way. I was learning so much—not just about soldiering, but about life.

A few days after our mission, I happened to read the inscription on one of the plaques hanging in the dayroom. This one read:

> War is an ugly thing, but not the ugliest of things; the decayed and degraded state of moral and patriotic feeling which thinks that nothing is worth war is much worse. A man who has nothing for which he is willing to fight, nothing he cares about more than his own personal safety, is a miserable crea-

ture who has no chance of being free, unless made and kept so by the exertions of better men than himself.

JOHN STUART MILL

The full meaning of this suddenly hit me.

Of those who most value their freedom, many choose to sacrifice it willingly for a time in order to defend that freedom for the rest of America. Here in this elite unit, we were set apart and held to higher standards than most in order to be first among those to defend the freedoms of our countrymen—many of whom had no knowledge of or appreciation for our sacrifices. The fact that some people would abuse that freedom to do evil, or that some would be completely apathetic to our sacrifices, was irrelevant. The service we rendered was its own reward.

God had never promised me that pursuing His purpose for my life would be fun. Only that the pursuit would be worth it. I had always understood the Bible's teaching that by enduring trouble now, I was laying up treasures in heaven. But I was beginning to understand that service in God's army paid earthly rewards as well.

I was coming to understand that a soldier is simply there to do the dirty work that others cannot or will not do—in order to preserve for them the freedom to live as they please. Those who partake of this freedom may never know about the sacrifices that are part of the soldier's daily life. But that's OK. The reward for service comes not in recognition by others, but in the very act of servanthood itself.

A verse worked its way to the surface of my consciousness: "The greatest among you will be your servant. For whoever exalts himself will be humbled, and whoever humbles himself will be exalted" (Matthew 23:11–12).

I was learning that being a servant suited me just fine.

4

A Toothpaste Sandwich

Praise be to the LORD my Rock,
who trains my hands for war, my fingers for battle.

PSALM 144:1

The presence of a desire does not justify its satisfaction.
The presence of power does not imply that one should be guided by it,
blindly and without restraint.

WALTER TROBISCH

8 DECEMBER 1988

Cold. Wet. Hungry. Exhausted. This was my world.

Five days to go in the mountain phase of Ranger school, and I was halfway done. I'd been lugging my fifty-pound rucksack through the woods of North Georgia for so long that going anywhere without it was like running around the woods in my underwear.

At the moment, staying awake was my number one priority. We were lying in wait alongside a deserted and lonely stretch of the Appalachian Trail, ready to ambush the opposing force that was due to come by at any moment. We'd been here for over an hour, and the sick feeling in my stomach wasn't entirely from the travel-size tube of toothpaste that I'd foolishly eaten the night before—nor was it from the intense hunger that had driven me to such desperate measures.

There was a bigger reason that my gut was doing somersaults: I was in charge.

Ranger school is the Army's premiere leadership course. Its staples are the standard infantry patrol missions: recons, raids, and ambushes. The school is designed to teach men how to lead others under the most extreme and arduous conditions. But since the instructors aren't allowed to shoot at the trainees, they find other ways to approximate the stress of combat.

Since the early 1950s, the Ranger school has worked to perfect the art of stress amplification. This is accomplished through food and sleep deprivation, nonstop cross-country patrols, and grading the Ranger candidate on *everything* he does. Over the years, the school has consistently washed out about 70 percent of those who attempt it. Students are subjected to grand tests of endurance in three harsh environments: mountains, swamps, and deserts. Those who remain at the end of the roughly two-month course are awarded the coveted black-and-gold Ranger tab, to be worn on the left shoulder of the Ranger's service uniform. Only about one-tenth of one percent of Army soldiers earn this tab.

I attended the course as a private first class, or PFC. It had taken me one full year in the regiment to earn a slot to the school. Winter was purportedly the worst time to go, but you couldn't be picky. Successful completion of the course meant a promotion to specialist—and a new job as a team leader within my squad, along with a new level of respect from my peers.

The soft sounds of deep breathing that I could hear up and

down the line told me that if I didn't stay awake to signal the start of the ambush, no one else would. For this part of the mission, I was the patrol leader. I hoped the Ranger instructor who was grading my performance wouldn't count it against me if he caught one of the men sleeping. It wasn't possible to rouse them with a nudge or even a whisper, since we were spread out and any noise or movement on the ambush line is a sure way to compromise your position. So I let the men zone out on the line, hoping that when I threw the grenade simulator, they would instinctively follow my lead and open fire with blanks from their weapons.

I grimaced at how stupid I had been to eat my toothpaste. Wintertime rations in Ranger school were one and a half meals per day—a half meal more than the summer students received. But the cold sucked the calories from our shivering bodies fast enough to make it seem like we hadn't eaten at all.

Walking point on a patrol two nights before, I'd felt hungrier than I'd ever been in my life. When we got back to our base of operations at the mountain Ranger camp, I plowed through my whole allotment of rations for the day—and had nothing left for dinner. I decided to find *something* to eat. After seriously considering the caloric value of my daily allotment of toilet paper, I settled for swallowing the Colgate that remained in the travel-size tube in my ruck. Big mistake.

Not only did this not satisfy my hunger, but the desperate stunt made me lose out on much-needed sleep later that night from running back and forth to the latrine.

And now, lying on an ambush line, unable to see the men to my left and right, I had a sinking feeling that sleep was not a luxury I would get to enjoy this night either.

There were times when I felt predisposed to doing stupid

things, and the toothpaste incident was one of them. It was almost as if I was physically unable to stop myself from doing what I wanted to do, even when I knew it wasn't a good idea. Lack of self-discipline was maybe my greatest weakness, although I scowled at the thought of admitting it. After all, Rangers pride themselves on discipline.

All my life I'd been taught that God knows our needs and will provide for His children. And I believed it. Why then did it seem like I was constantly trying to wrest control of my life away from Him? This wasn't about the toothpaste, but that episode pretty much summed up the pattern: (1) Chuck has a problem; (2) Chuck tries to take care of the problem his way instead of trusting God to do it; (3) Chuck ends up in an even bigger mess than the one he started with. Would I ever learn?

WHY WAS I ALWAYS TRYING TO WREST CONTROL OF MY LIFE AWAY FROM HIM?

I shivered silently in the darkness, wondering how long it would be until the enemy column happened along. I really needed to succeed on this patrol. With this one successfully under my belt, I might have enough points to make it to the swamp phase in Florida, the next three-week segment of Ranger school. I wasn't looking forward to that nearly as much as I was the twenty-four days of R&R for Christmas that was promised between the two phases.

I had been training now for nearly two months straight, starting with the three weeks of pre-Ranger training at Fort Benning. Then had come the first actual week of Ranger school, "city week," which was almost entirely physical training and hand-to-hand combat—on only two hours of sleep a night. That week had been the toughest so far due to the physical demands. I'd actually nodded off a couple of times while lying on my back doing flutter kicks.

During city week we had all been assigned a Ranger buddy. I got paired with Philip Lear, a baby-faced soldier stationed with the Second Ranger Battalion at Fort Lewis, Washington. We became fast friends, as might be expected, since we would get into trouble if one of us was ever caught without the other. We covered for each other in hand-to-hand drills, taking it easy on each other as much as possible without drawing the wrath of the instructors. And we huddled together for warmth on especially cold nights, trying to get what sleep we could.

After city week our class was bused to Camp Darby on the outer reaches of Fort Benning. There we ran daily patrols and lived in the field. We took turns in leadership positions, but there was never any opportunity to slack off. At the end of each phase, the squad sat in a circle and everyone ranked each member according to performance—like the reality show *Survivor,* but without the million-dollar prize. Too many low scores from your peers and you'd be recycled, sent back to day one to start with a new class, which, in my opinion, was a fate worse than death.

I'd come down with a brutal cough during the last week at Darby, a cold that turned out to be walking pneumonia. Afraid of being kicked out, I refused to see the medic about it. Instead, I convinced my fellow students to cover for me by giving them some of my food, which was the school's only recognized form of currency.

After enduring two weeks at Camp Darby, we were taken up to Dahlonega, Georgia, to Camp Frank D. Merrill, the Ranger mountain camp. There we spent a week learning mountaineering techniques such as rappelling, rescue climbing, and knot tying. We slept in the fabled "hooches," clapboard cabins that bore graffiti from every Ranger class since the late 1950s. It was clear from the notes that not much had changed in the attitudes of the men who came and went through these barracks. They were now, as then, filled with youthful humor, pride in their unit, and hope in the future.

We were fed pretty well at Camp Merrill, treated to wonderful blueberry pancakes every morning in the mess hall, since the cadre didn't want us zoning out at the top of a ninety-foot cliff. The extra sleep and food were a godsend that helped me recover from my pneumonia—which had caused me to lose nearly fifteen pounds.

The next week we began patrolling again, learning the unique challenges encountered when trekking in the mountains, such as the dreaded mountain laurel that grew so thick even deer couldn't penetrate it. Get your platoon into a thicket of the stuff, and you were guaranteed a No-Go on your patrol evaluation—if your buddies let you live that long.

Unfortunately, it had rained nonstop for the last week. Cross-country movement became a matter of scrambling up through mud and slippery leaves, then sliding down the opposite slope. At night it got so cold that I had to knock ice off my pack more than once, not wanting to carry any more weight than necessary.

One day in particular had been especially brutal. We trudged into Camp Merrill just in time for breakfast, feeling half-dead from walking all night in the rain while trying to find our way back from a mission. We dropped our gear in a muddy formation in front of the chow hall and went inside, eagerly anticipating a plate of those famous pancakes. My buddy Lear and I went through the food line and then wearily set our trays down across from each other on one of the worn wooden tables in the corner of the dining facility.

While Lear dug into his stack of pancakes, I bowed my head

and silently said a short prayer. When I looked up, he was eyeing me, having stopped midchew.

"What?" I said.

"Nothing." He continued eating. "I was just wondering what you were praying for."

I grinned. "Dry weather. And thanking God for blueberry pancakes."

"Good idea! Thank Him for me, too, then."

"Thank Him yourself."

Lear looked at his plate and said, "Humph!"

"What?"

"It's just been a long time since I talked to the big Ranger in the sky. I guess I just don't see the point sometimes."

"What do you mean by that?" I asked casually, digging into my breakfast.

Lear's tone was dry, almost bitter, as he spoke through mouthfuls of sausage and hash browns. "I grew up Catholic. Went through confirmation class, the whole shebang. But as I got older, I started noticing how people in the church acted during the week. I started to get a bad taste in my mouth after seeing these 'Christians' treating others badly, spreading gossip, and not helping people who needed it." He put his fork down. "It just didn't make sense to me how they could go around believing that they were going to heaven just because they prayed and went to church. I finally got to a point where I couldn't stand to believe it anymore."

"I know what you mean," I said, nodding at a paper Christmas decoration of Santa hanging on the wall. "Sort of like being told you'd better be nice so old Saint Nick there will bring you a present. You outgrew the myth."

"Right. Something like that." He went back to his breakfast.

I took a sip of orange juice and said, "Third stanza of the Ranger Creed."

"What?"

"Recite the third stanza of the Ranger Creed."

Lear looked at me like I'd hit my head on something. "What does that have…?"

"Recite it."

He shot me a quizzical look. We had both recited the Ranger Creed nearly every day since the first day of RIP, over a year ago. He began delivering it from memory.

"'Never shall I fail my comrades. I will always keep myself mentally alert, physically strong, and morally straight, and I will shoulder more than my share of the task, whatever it may be, one hundred percent and then some.'"

"OK," I said, "in the last twenty-four hours, have you noticed anyone who wasn't mentally alert?"

Lear sopped up the syrup on his plate with his last bit of pan-cake. "What, besides me? Sure, pretty much our whole platoon."

"Right. Then you should quit Ranger school right now."

Lear's head jerked up, and he looked me in the eye. "What are you talking about?"

"Well, by your line of reasoning, we should have quit the regiment a long time ago. After all, if everyone isn't maintaining the standards, then they are really a bunch of hypocrites. The Ranger Creed must be worthless. But that isn't the case, is it? The Ranger Creed doesn't lose a bit of value because a Ranger fails to maintain its standards. It's still as worthy of our aspirations as ever."

"So you're saying I'm wrong to expect Christians to be good people?"

"Not at all. You should be appalled when someone who claims to be a Christian doesn't act like it. But what you can't do is throw out Christ with the hypocrites. He was the only person ever to live completely up to His own standards. To me, that makes Him worth following. The fact that some of His children haven't yet become like Him doesn't even leave a scratch on His integrity. It simply means that they're students, not the Master. Most people outgrow the myth of who Santa is. But what they need to do is grow into the truth about who God is. I'm not the perfect Christian any more than I'm the perfect Ranger. But that doesn't mean I'm going to give up and stop trying to get better. Fortunately, I don't have to be good to go to heaven."

Lear looked thoughtful. He was about to say something when a voice bellowed from across the chow hall, "Let's go, Rangers! This isn't a country club! We've got a parachute jump to make!" We all jumped up and headed for the door.

"Maybe you're right," Lear said as we left our trays on the counter. "Anyway, let's hope today's mission goes better than the one last night."

5

No Shortcuts

Do not pray for easy lives, pray to be stronger men.
Do not pray for tasks equal to your powers,
pray for powers equal to your tasks.

Phillips Brooks

By standing firm you will gain life.

Luke 21:19

Lear and I stepped back outside. The rain had let up, and the clouds were beginning to lift.

"Come to think of it," I said, "I wish the rain would keep up—so they'd cancel this jump. Then maybe they'd have to truck us to the assembly point and we could get a little sleep en route."

I was hoping to find a way to continue our conversation from the chow hall, but right now we had an operations order to attend.

"More'n likely they'd just make us walk," Lear countered.

After being briefed on the mission for the day, we formed back up as a platoon and then marched to a nearby field. Rows of packed parachutes were arranged on the damp ground in front of four helicopters. We quickly strapped on our chutes and stood with hands on helmets, waiting to be inspected by the jumpmaster.

An RI walked up—ever present clipboard in hand—and began to call us out into groups of eight, called "chalks." The pilots showed up in their green one-piece flight suits and began preparing the choppers for takeoff. We lined up by chalks on the edge of the field and, when the aircrews were ready, lumbered over to them with all of our gear strapped securely to our parachute harnesses.

Fifteen minutes later we were sitting four abreast in the door of the Huey, circling thirteen hundred feet above the smallest drop zone I'd ever seen. The wide-open spaces we preferred to jump onto didn't exist here in the southernmost section of the rugged Appalachians. The Army had apparently rented the only flat spot it could find in the area, to be used as a landing zone for our patrol.

It looked more like someone's backyard.

The jumpmaster behind us finally shouted, "Go!" and we exited one at a time in one-second intervals. I tucked my head and held on to my reserve chute, tightly packed and secured to the front of my parachute harness. The shock I felt as the static line pulled the chute open was pleasantly subtle compared to the violent jolt I usually experienced when exiting a fixed-wing aircraft. The planes flew at roughly twice the speed of the Vietnam-era helicopter above me, which was now heading back to base camp.

Checking to make sure my chute had deployed properly, I reached up for the steering toggles on the risers above my head. Below, a small stream with overhanging trees bordered that postage stamp of a drop zone.

But as soon as I turned my chute, I knew I was in trouble.

The icy wind gusting in my face was blowing me away from the drop zone, toward the other side of the stream—densely packed with trees. Landing in them would be undesirable, to say the least. An injury at this stage of the game would force me to recycle and start the entire miserable course over, something I wasn't prepared to even contemplate. I held the chute into the wind and prayed I'd make the drop zone.

The round MC1-1B parachute I was using had a forward speed of approximately nine knots. The wind must have been a bit less than that, since I was making slow headway toward the drop zone by holding into the breeze. At about one hundred and fifty feet above the ground, it looked like I was going to make the DZ after all.

Just as I started to congratulate myself, another jumper swept underneath me in his own desperate attempt to stay out of the trees.

He made the drop zone. I didn't.

The other jumper's canopy created a vacuum, causing my chute to collapse. Since I was less than the minimum two hundred and fifty feet required for it to reinflate, I plummeted to earth. Fortunately, my canopy caught in a tree, slowing my fall.

I dropped like a rock right into the middle of the stream. Suddenly waist deep in icy water, I scrambled for the bank. The shock of the cold water was only partially offset by my hot anger at the soldier who'd stolen my air. My rucksack was completely soaked—the perfect way to start off a week in the mountains in December.

The day went downhill from there, but only figuratively. The walking seemed to be mostly up. As I trudged, dripping, into the assembly area, I heard the Ranger instructor call out, "Two-forty-three! Front and center!"

I groaned inside, because I was student 243 and knew I had just drawn the responsibility of leading the patrol to our objective—and maybe farther, if the RI felt like it. Ranger instructors were known to be sadistic and devious on a good day, but once in a while you'd get one that had a sliver of compassion. I hadn't heard what this one was like.

I wasn't at all prepared. I'd pretty much coasted through the operations order and now wished fervently I'd taken better notes.

The RI looked up from his clipboard. "You're the new patrol leader. You've got five minutes to get them moving."

The man I was replacing stood off to the side. I hurried over to him for a rundown on the mission objective and our present coordinates. I chose Lear as our point man. Using the map and a compass, we calculated the azimuth we'd need to follow to make the objective. Then I went around and got the platoon up and into patrol formation—basically a loose single file in this terrain.

We were in a valley, and our objective was at least twelve kilometers away—over a mountaintop, down a ridgeline, through a valley sure to be choked with mountain laurel, and up a draw to the vicinity of the Appalachian Trail, where we were to conduct an ambush. Lear headed out with the platoon in tow.

I shouldered my wet rucksack and fell into the line of soldiers about midway between the first and last man. From there I hoped to be able to keep track of the patrol as it wound its way toward the objective. Looking at the G-Shock on my wrist, I noticed that it was just past noon.

As we trudged along toward our objective, I tried to routinely check the compass every few minutes and make sure we were still on azimuth. I also tried to keep a pace count, so I'd at least have some idea of how far we'd come in case the RI asked.

After a few kilometers we found ourselves laboring up a steep incline. When we reached the top, I called a momentary halt so that I could conduct a map check. Actually, I was hoping I'd be able to get my pulse to stop redlining, but I wasn't going to tell that to the RI.

The men turned outward and took a knee, facing alternately left and right in a tactical fashion. From the sound of their wheezing, it was clear that I wasn't the only one who needed a break. The last man in the patrol decided that he needed something out of his ruck, so he pulled his quick release and the pack dropped to the ground with a thud. I turned to the sound just in time to see the pack go rolling back down the hill, with its owner and everyone else staring after it in disbelief.

After a momentary silence, we all broke out laughing. Everyone, that is, except the man who now had to retrieve his ruck from the bottom of the hill. Even the RI was laughing, though we were supposed to be tactical. It really wasn't all that funny, but your sense of humor can get a little warped under extreme circumstances.

Lear came back to meet me, map in hand. "Look here," he said, pointing with a sodden toothpick he'd been chewing. "This ridge-line we're on goes due south, almost right along our azimuth. The walking is tons easier up here on top, so why don't we just follow the ridge?"

"Right," I replied, "but our route goes southeast. This ridge will get us off course—not to mention leaving us exposed. You know the old saying, 'The easy way is always mined.' I think we'd better stay on azimuth."

"OK, it's your grade," he conceded. "I just hate walking on the sides of hills. Makes me feel like one leg is too short."

"We'll just call you 'Eileen' from now on then," I joked.

"Eileen? Oh—I get it. *I lean*. Very clever. Did you make that up all by yourself?" Lear moved off to take point again, shaking his head and grinning.

"And don't get sucked off azimuth down the hill, either!" I called after him.

It is extremely difficult to walk a straight line in the woods on a level route, much less a steep one. Walking on the side of a hill is the worst, however, because everyone has the tendency to take the easiest route to the bottom. It's instinctive to follow gravity and slip downhill. A good point man, however, keeps this tendency in mind and takes measures to offset it by going around trees on the uphill side and keeping a close eye on his compass.

Straying a few degrees off azimuth might not seem like a very big deal, but on a long cross-country movement the cumulative effect of taking little shortcuts can put you far off your objective.

I'd often felt that downward pull in life as well.

I was reminded of something I heard Rooster often tell the church youth group: "Even the little decisions you make in life can have a large impact on where you end up." Rooster had become a real mentor and friend to me in the time I'd been at Fort Benning. We spent hours talking in his office at the church about how we are all predisposed to getting "off course" on our journey through life—so easily led astray by our sin nature.

> WE ALL HAVE THE TENDENCY TO TAKE THE EASIEST ROUTE—AND GET OFF COURSE.

Rooster liked to remind me that failure to keep focused on our biblical compass can have devastating lifelong consequences. This went double for young people like me, since time has a way of magnifying decisions, both good and bad. And since it was so easy for me to "slip downhill" morally, I needed to be extra diligent to take measures that would ensure I stayed on track. Rooster was easy to open up to about the issues I faced, and he always seemed to have helpful suggestions.

As we moved out again on patrol, I reflected on how often I was tempted to take shortcuts in life. I was often willing to take a quick-and-easy route when doing the right thing looked like too much effort.

One issue in particular came to mind: the warm-body syndrome.

Every soldier gets lonely. It's an occupational hazard. Sometimes the worst part of a mission is returning to the barracks. After the weapons are cleaned and returned to the arms room, the equipment accounted for, and the after action briefing given, the married soldiers go home to their wives...leaving the single guys to the Spartan loneliness of the barracks. We'd clean our areas, shower in the communal bathroom down the hall, then retreat to our rooms. Where loneliness would descend like a fog.

On deployments, the married men suffered the pain of being separated from their wives, an issue the single soldiers didn't have to contend with. But back in garrison, it was different. Married men had wives to go home to. Single guys didn't even have a home. Living in the barracks was like being stuck in an extended summer camp or minimum security prison, where no outsiders or guests were allowed on the premises. Our feelings of isolation were legitimate. To a great extent we really were isolated from anything resembling a a normal life.

Rangers in my unit dealt with this loneliness by various means and methods. Many guys turned to alcohol—the only drug that was acceptable in the regiment as long as it didn't interfere with one's duties. Others looked to the prostitutes or exotic dancers so readily available down on Victory Drive, just outside the front gates of the post. In the year that I'd been at the unit, I'd seen many guys succumb to this loneliness by going out and marrying the first girl they could find, just so they'd have someone to come home to. This trend toward hasty nuptials and the fact that we were deployed and/or training for approximately half the year contributed to a towering divorce rate in the unit.

I dealt with this issue in a number of ways—some positive, others negative. First, thanks to my friend Rooster and his wife, I started attending church in Columbus, and it quickly became a loving surrogate family to me. Second, I moved off post to room with my friend Mike, who'd found a job in town as a schoolteacher. Though the arrangement ate up a significant portion of my meager paycheck, enjoying the luxury of my own room and bathroom made me feel like a real person again.

Even so, I still struggled with the warm-body syndrome.

I had dated around as much as my schedule would allow but felt the need to get serious with one girl, perhaps wanting someone who would miss me when I was out in the field. About three months before my slot opened for Ranger school, I started dating a smart, funny, vivacious blonde named Jennifer.

I'd been thinking a lot about Jennifer lately. I missed her badly, of course, but I found that this time away gave me a little perspective. Separated as we were, I could step back and view our relationship from the outside, trying to take stock of where it was headed.

Jennifer and I had gotten off to a great start. We'd taken time to get to know each other as friends for six months before we ever started dating. A few weeks after we started seeing each other, I wrote this entry in my journal:

It's been said that when you meet the girl that you are going to marry, you'll know it right away. I know it doesn't always work like that. I hope, though, that the girl I marry will be just like Jennifer. There's so much to love about her. We talk about marriage, sure. We talk about everything. But if God wants me to marry her, I'm confident He'll have her around when He's ready for me to tie the knot. We've prayed together several times that God would stand between us, so that as we get closer to Him we'll be moving closer to each other, and if we fall away from Him, we'll be drifting away from each other.

Three months later, reflecting on our relationship from the emotional as well as physical distance afforded by Ranger school, it was apparent to me that we were getting off course. I felt like I wanted more from Jennifer than she was ready to give. After all, she was two years younger than me, halfway through her senior year in high school. What was I doing talking about marriage? Was I pushing her to get too serious? Was it simply because I was afflicted with the warm-body syndrome?

Jennifer deserved better than that, and it would be stifling her potential to let our relationship get too serious. Yet I was afraid that it had already reached that point, and that perhaps I was making a huge blunder—trying to assuage the loneliness my way instead of handing the situation over to God. And that scared me. I knew that grabbing the steering wheel away from God in a life moving as fast as mine was asking for His discipline—and that it would surely hurt when it came. This was an added stress I could have done without in Ranger school. And I had no one to blame but myself.

The desire for companionship wasn't wrong. After all, the

Creator Himself hardwired that longing into a man's heart. But you can't focus on your hunger and forget about your thirst—that would be as dangerous as it is stupid. I ached for a life companion, but I needed my relationship with God even more. Deep down, I knew that if I could just focus more on what He wanted—and less on what I wanted—my life would go much more smoothly.

But for the moment I needed to focus on passing this patrol.

6

AMBUSH!

Answer me quickly, O LORD; my spirit fails.
Do not hide your face from me
or I will be like those who go down to the pit.

PSALM 143:7

Life is not lost by dying; life is lost minute by minute,
day by dragging day, in all the thousand small uncaring ways.

STEPHEN VINCENT BENÉT

It took us the rest of the afternoon to make our way to the Appalachian Trail. One man moving cross-country can cover up to five kilometers an hour on flat ground. Mountainous terrain will reduce his speed to about three. An entire platoon of men moves even slower, and constant care must be taken not to lose anyone along the way. A break in contact is a sure way to get what is known in Ranger school as a "major minus," a black mark on your record serious enough to cancel out a successful patrol.

I'd also heard it was possible to get a "major plus," but no one ever heard of it actually happening. You could get a major minus for all kinds of things: a bad attitude, losing a piece of equipment, or sleeping on guard duty. A major plus, I supposed, required something along the order of throwing yourself on a live grenade.

The winter sun had dropped behind the mountains an hour before we got to our Objective Rally Point, or ORP. It acted as a funnel through which everyone would pass to and from the ambush site, a good method for keeping control of the platoon. I left the platoon there, the men crouching on one knee in a tactical formation, while Lear and I went forward to scout out the ambush area. We stumbled onto the well-worn Appalachian Trail, all but invisible in the dark, and began looking for an optimal place to set an ambush. I noticed the Ranger instructor following us at a discreet distance, dreaded clipboard still in hand.

Just then we heard soft voices approaching. Lear and I dropped silently to the ground and lay very still, all senses on full alert. As the voices drew nearer, I found myself suddenly sweating—not from exertion, but from fear that this was the very "enemy" patrol we'd been sent to attack. Had we been too slow getting to our rally point? If the platoon wasn't in position when the OPFOR passed by, I was sure to fail the patrol.

Seconds ticked away and my every muscle tensed. The voices were almost upon us. I hoped they wouldn't hear my stomach growling, because I hadn't eaten anything since breakfast. Lear had his eyes trained on the trail, a light gray line about ten feet in front of us in the deepening dusk.

Then we saw the sweep of a light.

A flashlight? Soldiers almost never use a flashlight in the woods for any reason, as they tend to make you a target. My mind was still working on this inconsistency when the small group passed us, only four people, all wearing headlamps. Hikers. A woman giggled. Her perfume wafted over to where I lay. Perhaps they'd gotten a late start and were hurrying to meet up with the rest of their group for the night. They continued down the trail, unaware of armed special forces lying alongside the trail.

I let out a muted sigh and looked over at Lear. I could see his grin even in the darkness. "I wonder if they have any food?" he whispered.

Hurriedly, we scouted out a suitable site to emplace our ambush element, then headed back to the ORP and the waiting patrol. They stirred at our approach. Lear and I pulled the squad leaders aside, briefing them on our plan of action. I was probably burning more calories than I had consumed that day by worrying about the RI standing over my shoulder as I gave out instructions. The squad leaders were allowed two minutes to relay their part of the mission to their people. I designated two men to stay behind at the ORP and guard everyone's rucksacks, then prepared to lead the platoon back to the ambush site, about two hundred meters away.

It took about half an hour to get everyone into the ambush site. About fifty meters from the trail, we slowly crawled into position. Moving forward in the dark, I could hear the men on my left and right slithering through the underbrush, which wasn't a good thing, but there wasn't anything I could do about it. Once in place, we quietly camouflaged ourselves with leaves, pine boughs, and other castoffs of the woods, then settled in to wait for the enemy to appear.

As the sweat cooled on my uniform, I began to get chilled. I lay prone on the soft, damp humus of the forest floor, listening for sounds of the enemy patrol.

And my mind started to drift.

It promised to be a miserable night, and my spirits sank with my body temperature. Feelings of negativity engulfed me. *How could I be expected to lead men who were, like me, little more than malnourished zombies?* Frankly, I didn't trust some of the soldiers in my platoon. Most of them were officers and had come from non-Ranger units all across the Army. They didn't owe me anything. I was about the only one who cared whether I passed this patrol or not. Most of them were probably taking this opportunity to catch up on their sleep, knowing that if the ambush failed, it would all come down on my shoulders.

I trusted Lear implicitly because he was my Ranger buddy, and with all we'd been through, I felt sure he'd do what he could to help. If only my grade didn't rely on all those other guys, who were surely more concerned with their own performance evaluations.

Why I was doing this, anyway? Was that little cloth tab worth all this misery? Was this the ultimate ego trip, some crazy attempt to prove myself to the world? It had already taken a huge toll on my body, and for what? They certainly weren't teaching us any high-speed special operations tactics. The greater part of this course so far seemed to revolve around stumbling through the woods in the middle of the night. What was the point?

I thought of the well-meaning letters that Jennifer and my family had sent me. I was glad to receive them, but in one sense they served only to heighten my sense of loneliness. From this vantage point, my loved ones seemed to exist in a completely different plane of reality, almost as if my life back at home had belonged to someone else. I had been in this purgatory for so long that it was difficult even to remember what it was like to have a comfortable night in a real bed or a nice conversation over a sit-down dinner. I tried to conjure up happy memories in my head, but all that appeared were images of Twinkies and pizza, making my stomach rumble even more.

Come to think of it, God seemed pretty far away as well, even though I'd been defending Him to Lear that very morning. It was difficult to pray here, partly because we never had any time alone, but also because it felt almost as if God had taken a vacation and wasn't around to listen. Not to mention that I was afraid I'd fall asleep the second my eyes closed.

Perhaps the hundreds of kilometers we'd hiked through dark forests and smelly swamps made it feel like I'd left God behind somewhere. This, of course, couldn't be true; I knew God was with me, but I couldn't recall a time when I had ever felt His presence less than I did now. Was it the lack of food? the overpowering fatigue? the stress of making the grade and the fear of failing? Something—or a combination of somethings—had brought me to this low point in my spiritual life. My body might have been in the mountains, but my spirit was in a desert.

Just then a story from the Bible popped into my mind. I thought about how Jesus spent those forty days in the desert—just before Satan tied into Him with a barrage of temptations. He'd been forty days without food—and I was beginning to get a sense of what that must have been like.

Why had He done it? Was it a rite of passage of some sort? He could have come back home after a few days, and it could have ended as a fun camping trip. Why did He stay out there for over a month? It must have been worth it to Him somehow. I knew Jesus understood better than I did the fact that the most profound growth always comes in times of hardship. I recalled how the devil had tempted Jesus to turn the stones into bread to allay His hunger. Then Satan again tempted Christ by telling Him to escape His misery by jumping from the temple wall and being saved by the angels. Finally, Satan tempted Him with power and fame. Each time, Jesus passed the test set before Him and chose the more difficult path. By doing so, He came out of the desert ready to begin His ministry and pursue the mission He had come to accomplish.

Though I guessed that I'd already failed the food test by trying to make a meal out of toothpaste, I started to feel that perhaps I was here for the same reason. This rite of passage wasn't about being able to wear the black-and-gold Ranger tab or to boast about my exploits. Facing this kind of misery was the only way to build the kind of character that would make me qualified not only to lead other Rangers, but also to accomplish whatever it was that God had in store for me.

JESUS CAME OUT OF THE DESERT READY TO PURSUE THE MISSION HE HAD COME TO ACCOMPLISH.

My mother used to tell me, "Charlie, God never wastes anything." Remembering that truth improved my mood a little. It also helped to know that Jesus had been through His own sort of Ranger school. He knew misery and didn't shy away from it. But once Christ had passed His tests and sent the devil packing, didn't God send angels to minister to His Son? I could have used some ministering spirits right about then!

But the misery wasn't the worst of it.

My greatest fear was simply failure.

I knew that I wouldn't quit, because I'd made the solemn decision to exclude that as an option from the start. Success had become something of an obsession, really. So far, I had never fallen out of a run, a road march, or anything else. It was a track record that had quickly become self-perpetuating. I had seen what flunking out of Ranger school did to other guys in the unit, and it was clear that if

I didn't make it, the failure would haunt me for the rest of my life. The last five men to be sent to this school from my platoon had failed. My platoon sergeant had expressed doubts about my ability to do any better, and his words served to motivate me more than almost anything else. No, I would do whatever it took to pass this course the first time through.

The muted sound of a twig snapping on the trail brought me out of my reverie. My heart hammered in my chest as I detected movement through the trees. I quietly picked up the grenade simulator and got ready to pull the fuse. If this was another group of nighttime hikers, they were going to be in for a big surprise. Then the moving shadows materialized into soldiers as they drew nearer. They were conversing softly as they walked. I counted seven of them, carrying rifles. I held my breath as they walked toward the kill zone—then pulled the fuse and lobbed it out onto the trail. I grabbed for the M-16 beside me and shut my eyes tight in order to preserve whatever night vision I could when the simulator detonated.

Boom!

For a second, the forest turned to daytime as the charge exploded. The grenade simulator, equivalent to about an eighth of a stick of dynamite, exploded just in front of the group of OPFOR, sending them reeling. I immediately opened up with my M-16 on full auto. The blast violently awakened any of my classmates who had been dozing, and they quickly added their weapons to the cacophony. When the big M-60 machine guns started hammering away on our flanks, their sizable muzzle flashes illuminated the kill zone, revealing the OPFOR soldiers lying on the ground, attempting to return fire. After about thirty seconds of exchanging blanks, however, they chose to be dead—no doubt so that we could all go home and get some sleep.

I called a cease-fire and, when the shooting finally stopped, called out, "Search team, go!" I had designated Lear and another man as the search team. Their job was to go and check the enemy soldiers for anything of use to us and get a quick inventory of their weapons and equipment. As they did so, I prepared to get the platoon back to the ORP. "Demo team, go! The rest of you, get ready to move!" I heard Lear saying something to one of the "dead" soldiers lying on the trail as the two-man demolition team moved onto the trail.

In a few minutes, the search team returned to report what they'd found. "We got some maps and other intel. The demo team is preparing a 'notional' charge to blow the weapons and gear in place," Lear said. He leaned close to my ear and continued in a whisper, "And Holton, I got something even better from one of them—a Snickers bar!"

I gave him an incredulous look. "No way! You are my very best friend. Have I told you that?"

His mischievous grin practically lit up the forest. "Who says you're getting any?"

The squad leaders reported. They were ready to move.

"Let's move then," I said, and the platoon started filing past me. I counted each man to make sure that we didn't leave anyone behind. When the last security team that had been guarding our flanks was accounted for, the two demo men called out "Fire in the hole!" to let us know they'd ignited the fuse that would destroy the enemy weapons. They came sprinting past me, and I turned and followed them to the ORP. When I arrived, the men were already rucked up and ready to move. Everyone was anxious to get to the patrol base, where we would spend what was left of this night—and maybe get a little sleep. I calculated that we had eight kilometers to walk in order to get there.

"Ranger 243, over here!"

It was the RI calling me. Time to find out if I had passed the patrol. I headed over to where he was seated on a stump, a red-filtered Mag-Lite clenched between his teeth, as he checked his clipboard.

I stood in front of him as we discussed how the mission had gone. He cocked his patrol cap back on his head and consulted his notes with his flashlight. "The movement went fairly well," he began, "though you could have had a little better security out while crossing danger areas. You made it up on the leader's recon, though. For a minute I thought you were going to shoot those hikers. That actually happened last week with Fourth Platoon. They ambushed a man and his wife who were walking the trail after dark. Threw grenade simulators at them and everything." He added with a smirk, "I think the old man almost had a heart attack."

"Who? The hiker, Sergeant?" I asked, trying to stifle a laugh.

"No, the company commander! He wasn't happy having to explain that one to the colonel!"

"I bet."

Lear, who had been standing behind me eavesdropping, was trying to stifle his laughter. The RI waved him away and continued, "Anyway, you set the ambush and got the men into position on time. But they could have been a little quieter about it. Sounded like a platoon of tanks."

"Hooah, Sergeant. We could have done that better."

"Oh, and it's a good thing you used that grenade simulator, or some of those guys might have slept through the ambush."

I winced, but he continued. "All in all, I'm giving you a Go for this patrol."

I tried not to grin and forgot about the cold. "Thank you, Sergeant."

The RI called out another student number, designating that man as the new platoon leader. I took a moment to show him where we were and where the patrol base was, and just like that, the pressure of leadership transferred to his shoulders. I was only a grumby again. I gladly retrieved my ruck and fell into the end of the formation behind my Ranger buddy as we moved out.

Patrolling at night isn't complicated. While movement during the daytime requires walking in a wedge formation by teams, at night everyone simply follows the man in front of him in a single-file line. The objective is to stay far enough apart so that branches bent back by the first man don't whack the second man off his feet, but close enough together so that the man behind can see the glow-in-the-dark "cat eyes" sewn onto the back of the front man's rucksack and patrol cap.

We followed no trails and never used a flashlight. In the regiment we'd sometimes have night-vision equipment, but not here in Ranger school. I was often amazed at how well I could see in the dark once my eyes fully adjusted. Communication was done solely with hand signals, since talking could compromise the mission.

On a night patrol, however, it's easy to start following the man in front of you on autopilot, with everyone automatically following the point man. We sometimes joked that if the guy on point accidentally walked off a cliff, the whole platoon would follow.

I walked at the rear of the platoon, the swaying rucksack in front of me lulling me into its rhythm. With the pressure of leadership off my shoulders, I started losing the battle to stay alert. On previous patrols, this was where the lack of sleep really caught up to me. More than once I had actually started to hallucinate. My brain would decide, "You can keep walking if you want, but I'm shutting down!" I would start dreaming with my eyes open, superimposing things that weren't there over the reality before me. Once, during a halt, Jennifer walked up. I actually tapped my buddy on the shoulder and said, "Hey, there's my girlfriend!" like it happened all the time. Sleep deprivation does weird things to the mind.

I tried harder to stay alert this night, though. Especially since I was the last man in the formation. If I lost sight of Lear, I could easily lose the entire platoon and be stuck out here on my own. If that happened—and the RIs found out before I could rejoin the unit—I could expect a major minus. A break in contact is a very bad thing.

I walked along, weaving in and out of trees and stepping over downed logs in sync with my Ranger buddy's bobbing rucksack, and started thinking again about my relationship with God. Had I already experienced a break in contact with Him? Sometimes it felt like it. I'd carried around a small New Testament in my breast pocket for the last two months. But had I ever opened it? Even once? The Bible wasn't doing me any good that way. If I brought my compass along on a patrol but never took it out and consulted it, I wouldn't stay on course for very long.

No wonder I'm getting so depressed.

A Bible isn't a good luck charm any more than a compass is. Both are dead weight in my pack unless I take them out and use them. I also was coming to the realization that I needed to memo-rize as many verses as I could because it wasn't always possible to pull out a Bible and look up something. When I stopped to think how I'd attended church my whole life, it was shameful that I didn't know more verses by heart. I did remember Joshua 1:9, however, because it was written on a plaque that had hung on my wall for years.

Have I not commanded you? Be strong and courageous.
Do not be terrified; do not be discouraged, for the LORD
your God will be with you wherever you go.

That verse had been a comfort through much of what I had experienced in the Army. It helped me know that God was watching my back.

While these thoughts were running through my head, the platoon must have stopped, because I ran headlong into the rucksack in front of me. "Sorry!" I whispered, backing off a few steps. Lear didn't even bother to answer. Plowing into someone was a common occurrence.

I pulled the Army issue lensatic compass out of my breast pocket and checked our azimuth. It seemed to be OK. I wondered what the stop was for. I stood there for a few moments, checked my compass again, and then put it away. Getting impatient, I stepped forward to tap Lear and ask what was up.

But it wasn't my Ranger buddy; it was a tree.

Adrenaline flooded my veins as panic gripped me. The platoon hadn't stopped! I had walked into a tree and thought it was a Ranger. *Great*. Fully awake now, I dashed off in search of the column, images flashing in my head of the RI writing up a major minus, effectively canceling out the patrol that I had just passed. How could I have been so careless?

Fortunately, I ran into the column a moment later. They had stopped after all and were taking a knee, no doubt so the patrol leader could consult his map. I almost tripped over Lear—the real Lear, not another tree.

"Where'd you go?" he whispered. "Were you watering a tree or something?"

I took a knee beside him and grinned in relief. "Or something."

Exactly two months and one day later, I stood in formation on the parade field at the Ranger Training Brigade headquarters on Fort Benning. A weak afternoon sun shone through a high ceiling of clouds, and it was windy enough to drive the chill right through us.

Graduation day. The RTB commander was in the middle of his speech, going on and on about our accomplishments. I had expected this long-hoped-for day to be one of proud excitement. But somehow, it wasn't.

I just wanted it to be over.

I was exhausted to the bone; it was a tiredness that hung on me like old age, making it difficult to even walk upright. It was clear that this wasn't something I'd sleep off in a day or even a week. The persistent cough that had plagued me since Camp Darby was making it difficult to maintain my composure in the formation. All I could think about was getting through the ceremony without falling over, then going somewhere and eating myself into oblivion.

The longer the colonel's speech drew on, the more I resented it. Jennifer and Mike had made it to the ceremony, but I couldn't see them from where I was standing at parade rest in the center of the company formation.

In the last two phases of Ranger school, swamp phase and desert phase, I'd come to the point where it felt like I was going to be there for the rest of my life. I acquired a fractional sense of what the men who spent years in prisoner of war camps must have felt—the hopelessness of having nothing to look forward to but more misery. But I'd hung in there through the cold swamps of Florida and the frozen tundra of Utah's high mountain desert.

And now it was over.

At the conclusion of the commander's remarks, friends and family were allowed to come and pin the tab on their Ranger. Mike and Jennifer finally found me, and the sight of Jen was bittersweet. I had deduced from her few letters that these four months had been harder on our budding relationship than they had been on my body, and that was saying a lot. I had lost a total of forty pounds and looked for all the world like I'd just escaped from a Siberian prison camp. Actually, I'd fared pretty well until the last four days of desert phase, when most of our class had picked up dysentery from a tainted source of drinking water. It wasn't a weight loss program that I would recommend for anyone.

Mike shook my hand and said, "Congratulations, man!" Then Jen gave me a hug. She was a sight for sore eyes in a pretty blue dress. I had smelled her perfume from halfway across the parade field. It was amazing how living outside for so long had heightened my senses. After handing her the black-and-gold Ranger tab from my pocket, she fastened it to the left shoulder of my camouflage uniform with a safety pin.

And that was it.

I'd imagined this as one the biggest highs in my life. But it wasn't. I was just relieved to finally be finished. Ranger school had been the hardest thing I'd ever done, and if some guy had walked up at that moment and offered me millions to do it again, I'd have laughed in his face and probably punched him out for even suggesting it. At this point I was sure that the suffering I'd endured in

Ranger school would return to my mind daily for the rest of my life.

The course had been much more misery than adrenaline, but I suppose most rites of passage are that way. I had no idea how God would use these experiences later in my life, but I was convinced they wouldn't be wasted. I had a feeling that the most valuable thing I'd take away from the course wasn't tactical skill or technical proficiency, but simply the knowledge that God had still been there, helping me to persevere, even when it felt like He was far away.

Ranger school taught me more about myself than I ever wanted to know.

7

OVERWHELMING
FORCE

Trust in the LORD with all your heart;
do not depend on your own understanding.
Seek his will in all you do, and he will direct your paths.
Don't be impressed with your own wisdom.
Instead, fear the LORD and turn your back on evil.

PROVERBS 3:5−7, NLT

21 OCTOBER 1989

My watch read 0228. Under a light rain, I shivered silently, chilled despite the heavy rucksack on my back. I peered through the mist-shrouded trees ahead, searching for something in the hazy darkness that would help me get my bearings. But there was nothing. Nothing at all.

It was late October, and I was walking point for our squad on a nighttime patrol across the vast northern training area of Fort Benning, Georgia. It was slow going, and my frustration grew by the moment. It seemed like every square foot of the one-hundred-and-eighty-two-thousand-acre base we traversed was either swamp or thicket. We were running behind schedule, and if I didn't find a way to pick up the pace, our squad was going to be late for the scheduled rendezvous with the rest of Second Platoon.

To make matters worse, there were "enemy" about. An infantry unit had been assigned to act as the opposing force for this training exercise, and they were sure to have patrols out looking for us.

It seemed like we should be moving uphill to my left, but the compass in my hand said otherwise. I shook it lightly and turned myself in a circle to make sure the needle wasn't stuck. It spun freely. Part of me knew that it was right, but another part didn't want to believe it. I really *felt* that we should bear off to the left.

With no visual cue to back up the feeling, however, I knew that following my gut would be foolish. I'd been on enough patrols to know that you couldn't win an argument with a compass. To ignore the only fixed point of reference available was a sure way to end up walking around in circles for the rest of the night.

I checked the azimuth again and then, with a nod to the rest of the squad behind me, stuffed the compass back in my pocket and stepped off into the gloom.

Just recently I had learned that the need for a fixed point of reference wasn't exclusive to infantrymen. About a week earlier, we'd undertaken a mission at Fort Benning's urban training site, a little cinderblock village we called the MOUT site. MOUT stood for Military Operations in Urban Terrain. The mission had been to take over the central building in the town and secure the roads leading to it.

The entire company took part, and it took six helicopters, precisely coordinated, to insert everyone simultaneously. My squad had been given the job of landing on the roof of the building and clearing the top two floors. To do this, we rode an MH-6 "Little Bird" helicopter, flown by highly trained Night Stalker pilots. Each Little Bird carried three men on either side of the aircraft, sitting on metal benches attached there. Riding these while clinging to the outside of the aircraft was one of the most heart-stopping thrills I had ever experienced.

For the mission, we would race in over the treetops with the rest of the mission aircraft, then split off and fly into the MOUT site, firing our weapons off the skids as the craft alighted on the roof of the target building. The rest of the company secured the outside of the target building, while we began clearing it from the roof down, hoping to flush the bad guys out the exits on the first floor, where our comrades could take care of them.

When it came time for the mission, the opposing forces set burning tires at various points around the building. As our aircraft swooped in to land on the roof of the target building, Rangers were already fast-roping out of Black Hawks onto the street in front of it.

The helicopters were stirring up large amounts of thick black smoke as we stepped off the Little Bird, and I was confused to see one of the Black Hawks break procedure by turning suddenly and flying away, without dropping the ropes that hung from either door. Seconds later, my confusion turned to horror as I noticed one of our guys still hanging from the rope! It looked as if the pilot had made a potentially deadly error by not making sure everyone was clear of the fast-rope before leaving. I cringed as the line was dragged through the limbs of a nearby tree and emerged on the other side... without the unlucky Ranger. I breathed a quick prayer for that man's safety even as anger welled up inside me at the inept pilot.

But the mission went on, and we turned to the task at hand.

It wasn't until the mission was over, during the after action review, that I found out who the man had been—Specialist McDonald from First Squad. My prayer had been answered, and he had escaped with only minor cuts and bruises. The limbs of the tree had actually saved him from a twenty-foot drop to the ground. It was during the debriefing that I also found out why the pilot had left prematurely. The billowing smoke had obscured his vision momentarily, and without a point of reference by which to gauge his position relative to the nearby buildings, he had no choice but to pull out. Attempting to maintain a hover without a fixed point of reference was a quick way to lose a helicopter and its crew.

Later, as I thought back on that harrowing incident, I began to feel like that chopper pilot and I had some things in common. It's easy to lose your way without a fixed point of reference. And it's dangerous to keep blundering on ahead when you really don't know where you are or where you're going.

In my more reflective moments, I had to acknowledge that I needed to take a more active role in pursuing spiritual growth. Now that I was out on my own, there were no parents to wake me up for church on Sunday morning, keep tabs on where I went, and monitor the types of things that went into my mind. Now it was all my own responsibility, and while that prospect was a bit scary, it also had awakened in me a hunger to learn more about *why* I believed what I did. The answer "Because that's what Christians believe" no longer satisfied my intellect, as it had when I was younger.

I had been battling doubts about several issues. For example, whose truth was the right one? It seemed that everyone had his or her own definition of it, and I had begun to question how my version of right and wrong could be correct, while someone else's version of truth could be incorrect. How could anyone claim with certainty that his truth was any better than anyone else's?

Sometimes answers come from the most unlikely places.

It was during the after action review of our recent fast-rope mission, as we were discussing the chopper pilots' need for a fixed point of reference to maintain a stable hover, that the answer to my question appeared.

If a pilot tried to hover his aircraft based on his *feelings* about where the ground was, he'd soon be feeling nothing at all. If every Ranger in our squad decided to follow his own idea of where magnetic north was, we'd never reach our objective. It would be mass confusion, and we'd all eventually be split up—making it easy for the enemy to pick us off one by one. The mission can only get accomplished if we all agree to follow an objective standard, one that is consistent, predictable, and most of all, not subject to our wishes or feelings.

I finally came to the realization that my version of right and wrong *wasn't* better than anyone else's. And that was precisely why I needed to subscribe to a set of standards that existed independently of me or anyone else.

That realization led me right back to God's standards.

Jesus Christ provides the fixed point of reference that I need to maintain a stable "hover" in my life. He exists apart from everyone, including me. He came to earth and lived a perfect life, setting the standard for the rest of us to follow. The fact that not everyone recognizes His authority helped me understand why the world is in bad shape today. It was a tremendous relief to find that God wasn't afraid of my tough questions. If I was willing to do the mental legwork, satisfactory answers to those questions were out there, just waiting to be discovered when I was ready.

Cold water dripped off the bill of my patrol cap and ran down the green camouflage paint on my nose as I moved ahead on our azimuth. After a bit, the ground rose to an old, rutted tank trail. I brightened when I realized that it was going in roughly the same direction that we were. Perhaps we could move down the trail for a few minutes in the dark and make up some lost time. It would be safer to stay in the woods, but much slower. And I was really looking forward to getting this mission over with so that I could concentrate my energies on getting warm.

WHEN WOULD I LEARN THAT THE HARD ROAD IS ALMOST ALWAYS THE RIGHT ONE?

I moved back to Staff Sergeant Friar and quietly told him my idea. He shook his head vigorously.

"Are you hypothermic, or just stupid?" he whispered. Sergeant Friar didn't pull punches when it came to expressing his opinion.

"But we could make a kilometer in less than ten minutes, easy!"

"Sure we could, and we could get ambushed, too. You know better than that," he scolded. "Easy equals dead."

"Roger that, Sergeant." Chastened, I moved back to the point, skirted past the trail, and kept our squad in the woods.

Staff Sergeant Friar was right. I did know better than that. The chances of being ambushed were far greater if we took the path of least resistance. In combat, shortcuts can get you killed. That's why we went to such great lengths to make our training as realistic as possible. How many times would I have to learn that no matter how tempting it is to take the easy way, the hard road is almost always the right one? On a night like this, however, it took a supreme amount of self-discipline to keep from taking shortcuts.

When I was in basic training, the drill sergeants used to say, "Discipline yourself, or life will do it for you." Everyone knows that bad choices bring bad consequences, but the hard part seems to be getting that knowledge from the head to the feet. I rarely planned to do the wrong thing, but the breakdown between my intentions and my actions always came at the point of execution. I knew what I should do, but I couldn't always make myself do it. Or I had a hard time mustering the intestinal fortitude to deny myself the things that I wanted but knew I shouldn't have.

It helped a little to know that the apostle Paul felt that way sometimes, too. Mike had a New Living Translation of the Bible that I liked to read. In it, Romans 7:14–16 put it this way:

> The law is good, then. The trouble is not with the law but with me, because I am sold into slavery, with sin as my master. I don't understand myself at all, for I really want to do what is right, but I don't do it. Instead, I do the very thing I hate. I know perfectly well that what I am doing is wrong, and my bad conscience shows that I agree that the law is good.

In looking back at my own life's biggest failures and most painful disappointments, it was plain to see that nearly all of them could have been avoided—but for a lack of discipline on my part. My good intentions often seemed to fall to the weakness of my will. Were it stronger, I would have been able to make myself execute what I knew to be the best course of action. But whenever I made a habit of denying myself daily, forcing myself to do what needed to be done, especially when I didn't feel like it, I soon found my entire life in better shape than it was before.

We were nearing our linkup point, moving as quietly as possible through the wet, tall grass and scrub brush at the base of a small hill. A thicket loomed up ahead, and I changed course slightly to skirt around it. Suddenly, a noise exploded from the thicket as something burst up from the center of it. Adrenaline shot through my body as I dropped to one knee, weapon at the ready.

Two large deer bounded off into the night.

Checking behind me, I saw that the rest of the squad also had their weapons up and ready to fire. Eyes were wide behind camouflaged faces, but no one said a word. The only sound was the soft metallic clicking of weapons being returned to "safe." My heart rate slowly returned to normal as I stood up and kept moving, impressed that our training was so ingrained that the squad had acted instinctively when faced with a potential threat.

Linkup with the platoon went smoothly, and we snatched a couple of hours' sleep in the patrol base before the sun came up. By then it had stopped raining and was warming up considerably. Changing into a dry T-shirt made a world of difference in my outlook on life.

Our mission for the day was to set up a dug-in defensive perimeter on a nearby hill. The same OPFOR who had been tracking us the night before were supposed to mount an attack on the hill sometime after it got dark, so we had until then to fortify the perimeter. After a quick breakfast of cold MREs (meals ready to eat), we got to work, digging foxholes and building bunkers, setting trip flares and filling sandbags.

Defense wasn't something that Rangers normally did, since our missions usually put us on the attacking side. So while most of us loathed digging, it was at least a change of pace. Everyone pulled together so that by midafternoon there was a tight, defensible perimeter of covered foxholes with interlocking fields of fire. Our demolitions experts even came up with some surprises for the opposing force that, though non-injurious, would certainly give them a memorable, interactive fireworks display.

Once the perimeter was complete, the waiting began. There were still several hours of daylight left, so the platoon rested in the late autumn sun, weapons nearby in the off chance that the OPFOR would be foolish enough to attempt an attack before sundown. Men gathered in small clusters around the bunkers, some talking and some napping.

I sat down with my back to a small pine tree and then jumped right up again when I spotted a nest of fire ants nearby. Georgia fire ants are nothing to be trifled with. Inadvertently sitting on one of their anthills has been known to cause spontaneous, profanity-laced yodeling and world-speed-record attempts at dancing the macarena.

After a cursory check of my clothing to make sure I hadn't picked up any of the vicious pests, I walked over to my rucksack and pulled out a book that Mike had recommended recently, C. S. Lewis's classic *Mere Christianity*. It was the first time that I'd ventured beyond Lewis's children's stories, but those I had greatly enjoyed, and so was willing to give his apologetic works a try. I'd worked my way through the first several chapters the week before while waiting for an aircraft to get fixed so that we could perform a training mission. I'd been impressed by Lewis's talent for illuminating deep spiritual truths with simple word pictures, and had been looking for an opportunity to read more.

After retrieving the book, I found a spot next to a bunker that was free from fire ants and began to read. A bit later, Specialist

Rogers, a team leader from Second Squad, came over and sat down near me.

"Hey, Holton, whatcha readin'?" he asked, munching on a chocolate-covered cookie from his MRE.

I looked up. "Oh, C. S. Lewis. Do you know him?"

He chewed thoughtfully. "Hmm, sounds familiar."

"He wrote *The Lion, the Witch and the Wardrobe* and lots of other books," I said.

"Yeah, I've heard of that. He's a Christian, right?"

"Right." I nodded, then asked, "You go to church, don't you?"

"Uh-huh. My wife and I go to the chapel here on post sometimes. We haven't really found a church family in town, though I'd like to."

"Well, this book was recommended to me by a friend. He said that C. S. Lewis was an infantryman in World War I."

Rogers looked intrigued. "Interesting. Did he write a book about it?"

"Not exactly," I answered. "But this part I'm reading now talks a lot about war and battle and stuff, as an example of what the Christian life is like."

"Really? Like what?"

"Well," I said, scanning the pages I'd just been reading, "let's see, he says that the world is at war in a spiritual sense, and…oh, here it is." I began reading a portion of the chapter aloud.

But [Christianity] does not think that this is a war between independent powers. It thinks it is a civil war, a rebellion, and that we are living in a part of the universe occupied by the rebel.

Enemy occupied territory—that is what this world

is. Christianity is the story of how the rightful King has landed, you might say landed in disguise, and is calling us all to take part in a great campaign of sabotage.

Rogers cut in, "That's awesome!"

"Yeah, and there's more." I turned the page, skimmed a bit, and then continued reading.

He is going to land in force; we do not know when. But we can guess why He is delaying: He wants to give us the chance of joining His side freely... fallen man is not simply an imperfect creature that needs improvement; he is a rebel who must lay down his arms.

God will invade. It will be too late then to choose your side. There is no use saying you choose to lie down when it has become impossible to stand up.... Now, today, this moment, is the chance to choose the right side. God is holding back to give us that chance. It will not last forever.

Rogers was grinning. "Wow. You can tell he was a soldier."

"You sure can. If you want, I'll let you read the rest of the book when I'm done."

"I'd love to," Rogers answered.

Staff Sergeant Friar was moving our direction, and I could tell that he wanted something. "Looks like Sergeant Friar has a job for me," I said, putting the book back in my ruck.

"OK," Rogers said. "Talk to you later."

I picked up my weapon and went to meet my squad leader. "The platoon leader wants us to do a recon before it gets dark," he said, producing a map. "You and Stoner take Lavoie and do a loop around the south side of the hill. Look for the most likely routes that the enemy will want to use to approach the hill. The sun goes down in a little over an hour, so be back before then."

"Roger that, Sergeant. Do a loop around the south side, look for approach routes, back in an hour," I repeated.

"You got it."

I turned and went to collect Lavoie and Stoner.

Ten minutes later we were outside the perimeter, moving through the woods at the base of the hill. The three of us proceeded as quietly as possible, alert for any sign of an enemy reconnaissance party. We communicated easily with hand signals and body language, something that came naturally after having done quite a few missions like this together.

As we advanced, I thought about the conversation that I'd just had with Specialist Rogers. I made a mental note to see about getting him and his wife plugged into a church in our area. It didn't necessarily have to be the one I went to, because I knew they lived in South Columbus. I also knew little about my church's young married program. The important thing was to help him find someplace where he could get involved and feel comfortable and encouraged.

I thought about another part of *Mere Christianity* that I had read earlier that day, where Lewis asserted that church is like the place where the resistance movement meets to listen to secret messages from the commander. That is why the devil wants so badly to keep us away from church.

In the case of Christians in the Army, he didn't have to try too hard.

Hard training during the week often made "I'm too tired to go to church" an all-too-tempting excuse. I understood, however, that there was strength in numbers. It was a concept that the Rangers practiced religiously. We tried never to make an assault on an objective, if we could help it, without bringing a numerically superior force with overwhelming firepower.

In defensive mode, as we were tonight, our entire strategy revolved around interlocking fields of fire. Every bunker was designed with firing ports looking sideways, with fields of fire covering the front of the bunkers on either side. Those bunkers, in turn, covered the front of our bunker. One fighting position alone could be easily overrun, but a well-dug-in unit arranged where everyone covered each other was a force to be reckoned with. It made sense that resisting the devil and pursuing God's purposes would be best accomplished the same way—as part of a tightly knit group.

Forty minutes later, Stoner, Lavoie, and I reentered the perimeter and reported our findings to the lieutenant. An hour after that, we hunkered in our foxholes as dusk faded into night.

The attack didn't come until almost 2300 hours.

When it did, we were ready.

8

MISSION, MEN, THEN ME

You chart the path ahead of me and tell me where to stop and rest.
Every moment you know where I am.

PSALM 139:3, NLT

SATURDAY, 8 APRIL 1989, 0200 HOURS

"Specialist Holton, wake up!"

I opened my eyes but it didn't seem to make much difference. The moonless sky was as black as the inside of a waterproof bag. I would have thought that the whispered voice was a dream if a hand hadn't been gently shaking me.

Instinctively, I reached for my rifle as I sat up, trying to get my bearings after only two hours of sleep. Two hours more would have been nice. A throbbing pain in my left shoulder made me wince.

"What's up?" I said groggily.

"Guard duty, Specialist."

It was Private Lavoie, his silhouette barely visible in the shadows of the pine forest where we had made our patrol base. "You're up next."

"Hooah," I grunted, looking around. "Anything happening?"

"Not a thing. It was all I could do to keep my eyes open for an hour."

"Got it. Get some shut-eye." I hit the button to illuminate the dial on my watch. Now it was my turn to spend an hour trying to stay awake. The night was cool but comfortable, the air clean-smelling from the recent rain. It would have been wonderful to enjoy the starry view while sitting around a campfire somewhere—and then retire to a warm sleeping bag inside a tent.

But tonight there would be no tents and no campfires. We'd just begun a three-day field problem, a yearly exercise that culminated with a live-fire assault on Norwatt Hill, one of the more remote ranges on the northern section of Fort Benning. The closest thing to a sleeping bag that I'd ever carried in the Army was the trusty poncho liner that was still covering my lower body. Light and warm even when wet, it was, in my opinion, the greatest and most useful item the Army had ever issued—with the possible exception of jungle boots and hundred-mile-an-hour tape, the Army's version of duct tape.

I reached into my rucksack, which a moment earlier had been serving as a pillow. From it I pulled a pair of AN/PVS-7 Night Vision Goggles (NVGs). Our company had finally secured enough of the black monocular devices to issue three sets to each squad. They always came in handy, especially on moonlit nights, transforming the shadowy landscape into recognizable shapes, if only in a grainy, two-dimensional way. Flipping the power switch, I scanned the patrol base, noting the sleeping figures of our platoon spread out in a triangular perimeter, about thirty meters to a side. First, Second, and Third Squads made up the legs of the triangle, and Weapons Squad had a machine gun stationed at each corner. It was the standard way that Rangers made camp in enemy territory—completely tactical.

I was supposed to be watching for the enemy. Since this was training, however, I wasn't overly concerned about would-be attackers lurking in the darkness. I was more worried about staying awake through my shift so that I could wake up PFC Steadman, who at the moment lay unmoving five meters to my right.

Falling asleep on guard duty is about as close as one can get to committing a cardinal sin in the Army; in the regiment it is a sure ticket down the road. Now that I was in a leadership position, I had an even greater responsibility to uphold. If Ranger school had taught me anything, however, it was that I was capable of staying awake when I had to.

Keeping my mind occupied would make it easier. After peering through the NVGs for a few more moments, I thought of the journal in my rucksack. It usually accompanied me wherever I went, and times like this were good for catching up on my writing. It wasn't possible to turn on a light, however, since that would be a big no-no in a tactical patrol base. Then I remembered that the NVGs came equipped with an infrared illuminator, which worked over short distances and was invisible to the naked eye. I reached into the ruck for my journal and strapped on the goggles. After a bit of experimentation with the illuminator and the focus rings, I found that it was possible to read my journal. Writing was a little bit more of a challenge—kind of like trying to control your hand while watching it on television. After a moment, though, I got the hang of it.

Proud of my skills of improvisation, I began to record the events of the previous twenty-four hours.

We moved 12 km this morning after jumping into Mckenna DZ. What should have been a great jump turned out to be quite painful. We were jumping from Black Hawks at 3000 feet, a nice ride and something we don't get to do very often. I was the first one out, but when exiting, my left hand caught on Chester's rucksack and pulled him out with me. That yanked my left arm up behind me with a force that dislocated my left shoulder, I think. That was awfully painful, but it got worse. Since I wasn't able to steer my chute, it started oscillating badly as I fell, the weight of my rucksack making me fall like a brick tied to a helium balloon. I landed like a sack of wet cement, precisely on my left shoulder, and when the force of the landing slammed it back into place, the pain nearly caused me to pass out. I had to lie there for a while and decide if I wanted to walk away or be carried. Once it became clear that everything still worked, I reluctantly got up and dragged myself over to the assembly area, actually disappointed that I hadn't been injured badly enough to get out of this field problem.

Even before the painful mishap on the jump, my attitude hadn't been all that good as we left for the field. Jennifer and I weren't getting along, and there was little question as to why, though it was tough to admit. She was leaving for college soon, having enrolled at Auburn University, about an hour from Columbus. I could sense that she was looking forward to getting away from home to a new place with new possibilities, wanting to shed any vestiges of her old life: high school, parents...and apparently, me. It was becoming clear that she wasn't as ready for a serious relationship as I had perhaps hoped, and the more I tried to hold on to her, the less I succeeded.

It hadn't helped that I'd been gone so much lately. The unpredictability of my job had even caused me to miss a couple of dates we had planned. It was difficult for her to understand what I did, and I wasn't allowed to tell her much about it, since a great deal of our training was confidential. Also, having grown up around Fort Benning, her image of a soldier's life may have been somewhat tainted due to the endless parade of love-starved basic trainees on weekend passes that were a fact of life in Columbus, Georgia.

What Jennifer did know was that every training mission was keeping us apart, and just about the time that she got used to my being gone, I'd come back, and we'd have to start the process of getting to know each other all over again. For these reasons, it's possible that she perceived the job to be sort of pointless—grown men running around in the woods playing cowboys and Indians or something. She didn't really see the use of it. I couldn't blame her, either. Some of the training missions we'd done lately were making me wonder as well. Morale was dropping throughout the company. We seemed to have been out in the field nonstop for the last couple of months, ever since the new first sergeant showed up.

The Ranger regiment is legendary for its leadership, usually attracting the most dynamic of the Army's officers and NCOs. For those of us who had spent our entire careers in the unit, strong and selfless leaders were the norm. The culture of the regiment ensured that poor leaders didn't last long.

Most of us were hopeful that this would be the case with our new first sergeant—who seemed determined to make a name for himself as a hard charger. It might have been different if he'd chosen to lead from the front instead of being conspicuously absent whenever we found ourselves on a particularly nasty road march or field exercise. At any rate, our company was quickly tiring under the weight of his aspirations.

On the other hand, there was Sergeant First Class Kelly. He'd been the platoon sergeant for Second Platoon since I was assigned there a year and a half earlier. He and I didn't always see eye to eye on everything, and I sometimes resented his intimidating style of leadership, but none of us would have hesitated to follow him into battle. He was tough on us in the field but always right there with us, sharing in everything that we did. The first sergeant would sometimes follow us in his vehicle as we road-marched to the training site, but with Sergeant Kelly, if we were miserable, he was miserable.

It made all the difference in the world.

Poor leaders operate by the RHIP principle—Rank Hath Its Privileges. The Rangers taught that good leaders operate by the 3M principle: Mission, Men, then Me.

Even when I disagreed with Sergeant Kelly's tactics, I had to admit that his willingness to become like us earned my respect. He understood the value of setting a positive example and had the conviction to do so even when—*especially* when—it wasn't easy. Sergeant Kelly embodied the fourth stanza of the Ranger Creed:

> Gallantly will I show the world that I am a specially selected and well-trained soldier. My courtesy to superior officers, neatness of dress, and care of equipment shall set the example for others to follow.

Though I don't believe he was a religious man, Sergeant First Class Kelly taught me something about why God chose to come to earth to save us instead of simply pulling the trigger on Satan from His heavenly throne. He did it in order to identify Himself with us and make it easier for us to identify with Him. There is something inherently noble in choosing to put oneself in the line of fire to save a brother rather than simply warning him about it from a safe place.

Christ did even more than that. Not only did He make Himself like us so that believers could better relate to God, He put Himself on the line for the very people who were against Him.

Come to think of it, Christ would have made an outstanding NCO.

Some time earlier, my roommate, Mike, and I had been discussing this subject, and he pointed out a Bible verse that illustrated how Christ set the example for others to follow: "Christ, who suffered for you, is your example. Follow in his steps. He never sinned, and he never deceived anyone" (1 Peter 2:21–22, NLT).

> CHRIST PUT HIMSELF ON THE LINE FOR THE VERY PEOPLE WHO WERE AGAINST HIM.

The page in front of me was beginning to get blurry, not because the goggles were malfunctioning, but because I was starting to drop off. I put the journal and NVGs aside and quickly knocked out thirty push-ups in order to wake up and get the blood flowing to my cold feet. Only ten more minutes to go on my shift, then I'd wake up Steadman and get a couple more hours of rest before stand to.

The next morning we moved out as a platoon to Norwatt Hill. An hour later, we were in the middle of the most incredible swamp I've ever experienced. I got stuck in waist-deep mud several times and was kept from sinking only by the efforts of the man behind me, who had to pull me out by my rucksack. The swamp was only about a thousand meters wide, but it took us all of two hours to get through it.

Sometime during the crossing it began to rain.

It seemed like stopping only caused it to rain that much harder, so we tried to keep moving. What was supposed to have been a ten-kilometer movement must have been over twelve clicks, considering the "ground stretch factor"—my term for the extra ground that came with going up and down hills. My knees, ankles, and back were really starting to feel the effects of all the patrolling we'd been doing lately. I could actually feel my spine compressing between my shoulder blades. If this kept up, I'd be about four feet ten by the time my enlistment ended.

By 2000 hours, we had come to within a thousand meters of Norwatt Hill, where we set up a patrol base and began to prepare weapons and gear for the assault that would begin at 2300. I felt like a wet dishrag, and I couldn't wait to put on the dry T-shirt I had packed for after the mission.

By 2230, the team was all set and Jennifer was weighing on my mind again, when Staff Sergeant Friar returned from the leaders' meeting and motioned Stoner and me over to get an update on the mission. "OK, Sergeant Kelly just gave me a Frago on the attack," Staff Sergeant Friar began, referring to a Fragmentary Order, an update on a mission in progress.

"We'll be joining First Squad as the assault element on the raid," the sergeant continued. "Second and Weapons Squads will form the support element." He began sketching a diagram of the objective area in the sand with his finger as he spoke.

But other things crowded my mind as he laid out the specifics.

What tack should I take with Jennifer about her leaving for college? Should I try to convince her to stay with me, or should I let her go? Thoughts of her being invited to frat houses full of ogling college boys almost made me physically sick. *Doesn't she realize that no one will . . .*

"Holton, are you getting this?"

My attention jerked back to the moment. "Uh, roger, Sergeant." I lied.

"OK then," Staff Sergeant Friar continued, gesturing with his finger on the ground between us. "Once your teams have taken out all the bunkers on the east side of the objective, stay on the far side of the area until you see a red signal flare, then pull back with First Squad to the breach point in the wire, where I'll be waiting for you. Then we'll all move back to the ORP together."

"Hooah, Sergeant." Stoner and I grunted in unison then got up and headed over to our respective teams to disseminate the information. On the way, Stoner stopped me.

"Holton, are you OK? You're not acting like yourself today."

"Yeah, sorry." I answered slowly. "I've been a little out of it this week. Maybe I'm thinking too hard. I'll be all right, though." I marveled at how Stoner had been able to read me. But it shouldn't have been a surprise. Our squad spent so much time following each other around in the woods that we knew each other by the backs of our shaved heads, even in the dark.

"Just keep your head in the game, OK?" He said it in a voice that conveyed either concern or slight annoyance, I wasn't sure which. "I don't want you shooting me when I'm bounding in front of you." Tom Stoner was a very precise, detail-oriented person. If he hadn't joined the Army, he would probably have been an engineer or a Swiss watchmaker. He didn't like it when plans fell apart.

"Don't worry." I grinned at him. "I've got you covered."

Stoner didn't seem too sure about that.

As it turned out, he had good reason.

9

STUPID IN A
NO-STUPID ZONE

The heart is deceitful above all things and beyond cure.
Who can understand it?
JEREMIAH 17:9

It is hard to fight an enemy who has outposts in your head.
SALLY KEMPTON

Storm clouds gathered overhead as we moved out as a platoon at around 2300. Off in the distance, we began to see heat lightning, pink and blue and white, as we neared the objective rally point (ORP).

The platoon leader went on a reconnaissance of the objective, while we hunkered down on the side of a hill and watched the storm roll in. Soon the sky was flashing like a strobe light with the thunder constantly reverberating. This incredible light show went on for almost an hour, like God's own Fourth of July fireworks. The power and savage beauty of it all amazed me. *What kind of God has so much energy and creativity to spare that He would concoct something as profoundly beautiful as this lightning storm—only to blow it away a few minutes later?*

When the wind hit, I looked at Stoner and said, "We're in for it now!" A couple of minutes passed, and then we heard a sound like that of a jet fighter approaching. The roar got louder and louder, and we braced ourselves, feeling completely exposed on that hillside. Seconds later, a wall of ice-cold raindrops hit like an artillery barrage, and I was awestruck as the full fury of the storm engulfed us. Sitting in the open, however, served to, well…dampen the experience.

After the initial onslaught, it continued to drizzle until well past midnight, which provided perfect cover as we moved to the ORP, where the platoon split into the assault element and the support element. Support moved up on the east side of the enemy positions and prepared to lay down covering fire, while Second Squad joined ours in circling around to approach the hill from the south.

I couldn't remember the exact plan in this case, but I figured I could wing it since we'd done missions like this so many times before. At a preset time, machine guns would open up on the hill. Then, after giving them a moment to soften up the objective, our element would send up a flare signaling the support element to shift fire to the north, while we began moving across the enemy outpost from the south. We'd clear the enemy bunkers and trust support to keep shifting fire so that none of us would become friendly-fire casualties.

And that's what happened. Our assault team was in place when the support element began firing on Norwatt Hill. We advanced on it from the south, and with my NVGs I could just make out the silhouettes of sandbagged bunkers on the hill. When we reached the outer perimeter of the enemy base, we encountered a ring of concertina wire, razor-sharp barbed wire coiled up like the devil's Slinky.

The standard procedure for quickly crossing a wire obstacle was to have a private throw himself on it facedown, crushing it with his body while everyone else ran across his back. In this case, though, First Squad had come prepared with an aluminum ladder to drop on the concertina, much to the privates' collective relief.

Once the breach was prepared, a white flare went up, and the support element shifted fire. Our element made its way over the ladder man by man and then spread out in four teams that began working their way across in a line to the objective. There were at least three bunkers in my team's path. One additional bunker lay in the exact center of the objective, and I wasn't sure if we were supposed to clear it or leave it for the team on our right. It looked like the command bunker, so I figured whoever got there first would secure it.

We bounded quickly across the objective, clearing the bunkers by throwing grenade simulators into their firing ports and then going inside, firing blanks, to be sure that they were clear. Enemy soldiers were only imaginary this time. But we went through the motions anyway, as we had many times before.

What would Jennifer think if she could see me jumping into bunkers and firing pretend bullets at pretend bad guys in the middle of the night?

We reached the command bunker, and I yelled, "Chester, Lavoie, cover me!" Then I went charging into the sandbagged entrance, firing half a magazine of blanks as I entered. Once inside, I had just enough time to look around the small, dark room when I saw something bounce into the firing slit on the far side. It took another half second for me to discern what it was.

A grenade simulator.

I turned and dived back toward the door of the bunker just as the simulator detonated, its force magnified by the confines of the bunker.

But I wasn't fast enough.

The flash and shock of the explosion knocked me almost unconscious. Temporarily blinded, I staggered back out the way I had come just as someone from First Squad burst into the bunker's other entrance, firing wildly. Back outside, I bumped into Lavoie and sat down hard next to him, dazed. I could vaguely hear him yelling something through the ringing in my ears, but I wasn't sure if he was saying "What was that?" or "Are you OK?" I put my hand on his shoulder and struggled to my feet, trying to regain composure. At some point, I must have yelled, "Let's move!" because the team picked up and bounded to the far side of the objective.

A moment later, my vision had been sufficiently restored for me to see the red flare go up. We turned and moved quickly back across the objective to the breach in the concertina wire where Staff Sergeant Friar was waiting. Once both squads clambered back over the wire and retrieved the ladder, we made our way back to the ORP. My head was still throbbing when we arrived.

The support team was already waiting for us. Sergeant First Class Kelly made sure everyone was accounted for, and then we quickly picked up our gear and moved about a click to the staging area where we would be spending the night. I wasn't sure who had seen me enter the command bunker other than Lavoie and Chester. What had gone wrong wasn't entirely clear to me yet, but I knew I'd better find out before tomorrow's live-fire exercise. My ears were still ringing.

It was 0200 when we arrived at the patrol base. We quickly set up a perimeter, then implemented a sleep schedule. The aching in my head had almost disappeared by the time I sank into an exhausted slumber cocooned in my poncho liner.

The next morning the cooks from our mess hall showed up in

a large deuce-and-a-half truck with a welcome hot breakfast. Afterward, Staff Sergeant Friar came over and called our squad together for an after action review of the mission the night before. Before everyone else arrived, he turned and gave me a hard look.

"Holton," he said, "Sergeant Smith from First Squad wants to know what you were doing in the command bunker last night. He said Harrison almost killed you with a grenade sim."

"Roger, Sergeant, I don't know what happened," I conceded sheepishly.

"Didn't you hear me specify in the Frago that First Squad was going to handle that bunker?"

"Negative, Sergeant. I must have droned out during that part. It won't happen again."

Staff Sergeant Friar cursed and shot me a disapproving look. "It had better not. You screw up tonight and we'll be dragging your carcass off the objective to a medevac. You've been out in left field ever since we got out here. That's not like you. Wherever your brain is, go find it and bring it back. Deal with your problems on *your* time. Out here I need you to focus on the mission. The rumor mill is saying that we're headed down south for some training in a few weeks. Sounds like it's going to be a smoker deployment. I need you to have your stuff wired tight when we go. Tonight is the live-fire. No more mistakes, hooah?"

"OUT HERE I NEED YOU TO FOCUS ON THE MISSION."

"Hooah, Sergeant. Do you know where we're going, exactly?"

"Panama."

My heart sank. We had already been to Panama the year before for three weeks. The jungle was absolutely brutal. Three days in the field there was about like three weeks in a more temperate climate. The worst part about it, though, was that it couldn't have come at a worse time. This would do nothing to improve my relationship with Jennifer.

Sergeant Friar's disappointment hurt, but it was clearly a wake-up call. It was becoming clear to me just how dangerous it was to allow girl problems to steal my focus from the task at hand. When in mission mode, one has to compartmentalize, to shut the nonessential off in a separate room of the mind and relegate it to the back burner while focusing exclusively on the performance of mission-critical tasks. In combat, the ability to pursue the mission with a single-minded purpose was the key that would determine whether I—and possibly some of my buddies—returned home under our own power or in a body bag. As a team leader, I had the responsibility now to set a proficient example at all times. Ranger school had taught me that nothing inspires men like decisive and competent leadership.

Sergeant Friar had brought up another good point as well. The entire unit was affected by my mistakes. None of us had been issued a Lone Ranger mask. If I messed up and got hurt, I would be endangering the lives of my fellow soldiers. In addition, I'd be diverting their attention and resources from the mission, as they'd be forced to care for me. Beyond that, the unit would have one less functional weapon—which could mean the difference between success and failure.

It was no wonder that attention to detail and personal integrity were stressed so heavily here. Whenever any of us failed to execute our portion of the mission correctly, we instantly went from being an asset to a liability.

I made a firm decision right then and there not to think about

Jennifer any more until the field problem was over. While we were out here, it was unfair to me, my men, and my unit not to give "one hundred percent and then some," as embodied in the third stanza of the Ranger Creed. No matter what anyone thought, this training was no game. It had to be deadly serious because there are no second chances in combat.

The live-fire mission went well that night. The assault element was the most dangerous place to be: charging across the objective with tracer rounds from the support team kicking up dirt several yards ahead of us, trusting our buddies with the M-60s to shift fire as we advanced across the objective. The distinctive sound made by the incoming bullets was an eerie reminder that this was no game.

When the mission was over that night, we took extra care to clear our weapons and gear of any live rounds, checking each man at least three times. We left all live ammo with the armorer, who loaded it into a camouflage six-by-six truck to take back to the ammo point. Then we retrieved our rucksacks and moved out on patrol through the inky Georgia night.

Just before 0300 we made it to an old, abandoned cemetery next to a gravel road, where the buses were scheduled to pick us up and take us back to the barracks at about 0630. Rather than go into a tactical patrol base next to the road, Sergeant Kelly simply told us to lie down and go to sleep until the buses arrived, leaving one man on guard duty for the entire platoon. We were shocked because Sergeant Kelly almost never went anywhere without being "tactical"—we even joked about him donning camouflage to go grocery shopping. But we certainly weren't going to argue.

It began raining again, though only lightly. I wasn't excited about sleeping in the mud, especially when the prospect of a real bed was so close. After a quick look around, I noticed a few raised cement tombs. In Georgia, the water table is often too high to bury people six feet deep, so they are put into concrete boxes set only partially into the ground. And since I was much more tired than superstitious, I grabbed my gear and arranged myself atop one of the concrete coffins with my poncho draped over the headstone to keep the rain off. My sleeping habits hadn't fully recovered from Ranger school, so sitting down still had the same effect on me as hitting the "off" button. The sarcophagus might not be comfortable, but it was dry, and I went out like a tired kid in a car seat.

The buses arrived late, so when we made it back to the barracks it was already time for chow. We left one man to guard our equipment while the rest of us hurriedly ate, then we retrieved our gear and spent the next several hours getting weapons cleaned and turned in. The word had come down that we would be able to go home early if everything got done, and I was hoping that would be by about noon.

Not surprisingly, bureaucracy intervened, and we had to sit through a threat briefing on the world situation first. We were on Ranger Ready Force, Level 1, or RRF-1, which meant that if a crisis requiring our services arose somewhere in the world, Third Battalion would be the first to go. Each of the three Ranger battalions took turns on RRF-1, which meant that for a third of the year we weren't allowed to travel more than two hours away from base and had to be available by phone or pager at all times.

The classified threat briefings that were given once a quarter always interested me. It was astonishing how many things went on around the world that never made the news. At any rate, it was nearly 1500 by the time I signed out of the battalion. Twenty minutes later I was pulling into the driveway of the brown A-frame house that Mike and I were renting in Columbus. He wasn't home when I arrived, so I went upstairs to my room and got ready to go to the weekly Wednesday night activities at the church.

As I showered, the blank-fire mishap from two nights previous weighed heavily on my mind. I badly wanted to be a valuable part of Third Platoon, but the feelings of inadequacy I'd experienced as a private came flooding back—feelings that weren't welcome in my mind. Allowing personal problems to intrude on my concentration at work was certainly a recipe for disaster.

Something had to change before the situation with Jennifer got me injured, fired ... or worse.

10

AFTER ACTION REVIEW

Love is more stern and splendid than mere kindness.

C. S. LEWIS

The mind of sinful man is death,
but the mind controlled by the Spirit is life and peace.

ROMANS 8:6

I decided to go to church early in order to catch Rooster in his office before the evening's scheduled events. I hoped he'd have some advice on how to handle my relationship with Jennifer. Dressing quickly, I grabbed my pager and headed out the door.

Rooster was in his office when I arrived, putting the finishing touches on the night's youth activities. He looked up and smiled when I knocked on the frame of the open door.

"Hey, Chuck, we missed you Sunday!"

"I'd much rather have been here," I replied, rotating my still-sore left shoulder.

"Looks like whatever they had you doing, it didn't include sleep."

"I'll get plenty of sleep when I'm dead."

"That's one way to look at it." He gestured to the antique barber's chair that graced one corner of his eclectic office. "Have a seat."

"Thanks," I said, settling into the chair and leaning back. "Just a trim, please."

He laughed. "Sure. Looks like it's been, what, three days since you got it cut?"

"Only a hundred and two haircuts left before I get to be a hippie like you."

Rooster laughed and shook his head. "So can you tell me what you've been up to, or would I have to sleep in a vault for the rest of my life if you did?"

"Way too much sleeping in the rain, lately. But actually, I would like to talk to you about something."

"OK, shoot!"

"Well, it's about Jennifer. We've been seeing each other now for about six months, and I'm really getting attached to her. She's, well, she's just what I've been looking for in a girlfriend."

"So what's the problem?"

"Well, as you know, she'll be graduating soon and heading off to Auburn. I know she's excited about it and—I'm excited for her. But it seems like she can't wait to leave Columbus, and whenever the subject comes up, it seems like we get into a fight about it. I just can't help feeling that she wants to get rid of me, too. And frankly, the thought of her running around a college campus scares me."

Rooster put his pen down and rubbed his red beard. "Why does that scare you? Too much competition?"

"I don't think that's the reason so much as—well, it's just that

I'm afraid she'll be tempted to…you know, experiment with her freedom. Maybe go a little wild. There are some pretty crazy parties on college campuses, from what I've heard."

"So you don't trust her?"

"Of course I trust…" I hesitated. "OK, maybe not. I don't know. I want to give her the freedom to do what makes her happy, but I don't think she realizes what *will* make her happy."

"Which would be staying with you, right?"

I rubbed my stubbly head. "Of course. No one is going to love her like I will."

Rooster leaned back in his chair. "Let me ask you something. Are you honoring God in your relationship with Jennifer?"

I hesitated. Rooster didn't pull punches. "What do you mean? We pray together sometimes, if that's what you're asking."

"I'm asking if you're doing what's best for her—spiritually, emotionally, and physically."

That last one stung. I found myself unable to meet his gaze. "Well, we're not sleeping together, if that's what you mean. I won't pretend that hormones aren't a problem, though. We may have gone a little further than we meant to a few times."

"Uh-huh." He nodded slowly and steepled his fingers under his chin. "Look, you know you can be straight with me. Are you really serious about her, or is she just a convenient way to get your needs met?"

I bristled slightly. "I know I can be straight with you," I said pointedly. "I can't say that I've been the *best* influence on Jen, but my intentions have been good. I really love her, Rooster. I think she might be the girl that I'm going to marry. She's not just a portable make-out unit. I really do want her to feel good when she's with me."

"Chuck, if you love her, you'll do what's right for her, not just make her feel good. Have you ever heard the verse in 1 Corinthians that talks about what love is like?"

"Love is patient, kind, etc. That one?"

"That one. First Corinthians 13:4–7. The first thing that it says is that love is patient. Do you believe that God knows whether or not Jennifer is the one for you?"

"Of course He does."

"Then if she is, don't you think you can afford to let her go for a while and be patient, trusting that God will bring her back to you when the time is right?"

I was leaning forward now, staring at my feet. "I can, but it won't be easy."

"It never is. In the meantime, I'd venture to say that the reason you two are fighting isn't that she's going away. It's that you're becoming too intimate physically. I'm going to let you in on a little secret. When you embrace a girl, you aren't just touching her body, you are caressing her soul. She is becoming attached to you in spirit, and that's an extremely complicated and dangerous thing to do—especially when it's not in God's plan.

"The last part of that passage in Corinthians says that love isn't self-serving. If you are using Jennifer to get your needs met, you aren't doing her any favors. You are setting her up for some major hurt down the road, and that's not the loving thing to do. If you love her, you'll be more concerned about making her feel good *about herself*, not simply making her feel good."

I was feeling pretty convicted. "I've heard you say that before. I guess I'm setting us both up for a fall by letting it go too far. Maybe a little distance between us will be healthy."

"Sure." Rooster smiled. "Besides, haven't you heard the saying

'If you love something, set it free, and if it doesn't come back to you...'"

"...hunt it down and kill it?" I interrupted.

He laughed heartily. "Spoken like a true Ranger."

I wasn't done, however. "The other thing is that, since she's leaving soon, I want to spend as much time with her as possible, but work is driving me crazy! We're constantly out in the field or on deployment, and I can never tell Jen for sure when I'm going to be home, or explain to her what we're doing. It's had a negative effect on both of us. She just doesn't understand how important this job is. It's starting to affect my performance at work. I almost got blown up this week on a mission because I was distracted worrying about our relationship. I don't know what to do! When I'm on a mission, I have to be firing on all cylinders and can't afford to be preoccupied with thinking about girlfriends or anything else that doesn't pertain to the mission. With my head full of non-task-essential problems, I become a danger to myself and to the entire unit. I guess it's just more difficult than I thought to juggle a civilian life and an Army career."

I WAS FEELING PRETTY CONVICTED.

Rooster was serious again. "Hey, look, Chuck, welcome to the real world. It's not just Army guys who have those problems. We've all got to deal with the little urgencies in life. In case you forgot, your biggest mission is the one that you accepted when you became a Christian—to follow Christ. Satan doesn't have to get you to worship him directly. All he has to do is distract you from God's purpose. He does that by throwing obstacles in your path and by deceiving you into trying to get your needs met anywhere but in Christ. A guy has to learn to see things from the proper perspective—God's perspective—if he's going to be able to separate what's important from what's not. Fail to do so, and you're certain to become a casualty at some point."

"That's easier said than done."

"Of course. Is it tougher to get into the Ranger regiment than it is to become a cook in a regular Army unit?"

"You better believe it."

"Well, if you plan to follow God's purpose, you'll be real disappointed if you're expecting something easy."

"I guess you're right."

"Also, if you become a spiritual casualty, you put an added burden on your fellow soldiers in Christ. Say you get married and then a few years later leave your wife and run off with another woman. Your moral failure becomes a burden on the rest of the church, because now we've got to step in and take care of your family as well as our own."

"Good point. But what about Jennifer versus my job?"

"She's seventeen! Cut her some slack. If it's meant to be, she'll learn to live with whatever you do for a living."

Teens were beginning to trickle into the youth room outside of Rooster's office. I rose to leave. "I'd better let you get to work."

Rooster came out from behind his desk and put a hand on my shoulder. "Hey, this is work," he said with a wink. "Let me pray with you about this before you go."

"OK." We bowed our heads.

As he began to pray, a wave of emotion swept over me. I did love Jennifer, but my actions hadn't been showing it. Then he said something that made me wince.

"Father, I pray that You will look through Chuck's and Jen's feelings for each other, and if their motives aren't pure, please take the feelings away. It might be painful for them, but we know that Your plan is the best for us, and we want to do Your will."

Though it was difficult to ask God to take away something— or in this case, some*one*—I didn't think I could live without—I prayed along with Rooster for the strength to choose what was right for both Jen and me. When we finished, it took a moment before I could look up.

"Thanks, David," I said quietly. Calling him Rooster seemed too flippant at a time like this.

"Anytime, Chuck."

That night after church I gave Jennifer a ride home. We didn't talk much on the way, both feeling the tension that had been build-ing between us. I pulled to a stop in front of her house and shut off the car. A light rain pattered on the roof.

I turned to look at her in the passenger seat and said, "Jen, I need to apologize for being such a pain lately. I know you are excited about going off to college, and I'm excited for you. I'm just missing you already, I guess. It doesn't help either that I've been gone so much, but I hope it won't always be like this."

She brushed a strand of blond hair out of her face and looked at her lap. This was clearly difficult for her. "Chuck," she began softly, "I have to be honest with you. I've been thinking a lot lately about whether or not I'm ready for a relationship with a guy who is in the Army, a Ranger, and is always gone." She hesitated. "I came to the conclusion that, no, I'm really not ready. Neither am I ready for a relationship with any other guy. But…the fact is, I'm in love with you, and even though I'm not in love with your job, I'm trying to learn to accept it."

"I understand, Jen. I really do. I've been through the changes that you're going through right now. I think we've gotten ahead of ourselves in a lot of ways, and that's my fault. I could marry you in a minute, but…"

She shook her head. "I'm not ready to think about marriage yet. I'm seventeen years old, with the most awesome future ahead of me. You have to realize that when I go to college, life is going to be totally different for us. I'll probably go wild at first. I've got a lot of playing to do before wedding bells start ringing. Don't you understand?"

I nodded fervently. "I do! You're free to do whatever you want when you go. For the first few months that we were dating, it was fun to talk about marriage, but I know now that neither of us is ready for that yet. Frankly, I'd be quite content to let your parents foot the bill for you for a while longer."

Jennifer threw a smirk at me as I continued. "We've talked about this before. If God wants us to be married, He'll bring us together *when we are ready!* What happens between now and then won't matter much when the time comes. I just don't want you to be shortsighted. I know you hate my job, but who knows? A year from now I could be going to college full-time. I'm not going to be in the Rangers forever."

"I don't hate your job; I just dislike it at times. It all seems so useless to me. The only thing that I understand is that I live day to day thinking maybe you're in the hospital, or in the field, or a foreign country…that's a lot for a girl who's about to graduate high school to think about."

"You're right; it is," I conceded. "And as bad as the timing is, I just found out that we're being deployed again in a few weeks—sorry about that. I guess that doesn't help my case any."

Jennifer turned toward the window and didn't say anything. I reached out and took her hand.

"Look, I want you to have a great time at college. I'm not going to hold you back. I'll just tell you this one thing. Try to find someone who treats you better than I do. The ball is in your court. I'm choosing to love you enough to let you go. And I'll be praying for you every day. Will you also pray for me while I'm gone?"

She turned toward me, a tear rolling slowly down her face. Squeezing my hand, she answered quietly.

"I promise."

11

STRAGGLERS

And we urge you, brothers, warn those who are idle,
encourage the timid, help the weak, be patient with everyone.

1 THESSALONIANS 5:14

Carry each other's burdens,
and in this way you will fulfill the law of Christ.

GALATIANS 6:2

The pre-dawn darkness echoed with the sound of athletic shoes crunch-crunch-crunching on the gravel road in perfect unison. Thirty-three men ran in platoon formation, shoulder-to-shoulder in three columns, dressed in black from head to toe. A small red-and-white Ranger scroll just above the left breast provided the only color on each man's physical training (PT) uniform.

If Rangering were a religion, this would be daily devotions.

Whenever we were in garrison, PT was a daily fact of life, usually practiced for an hour or so before breakfast. The typical workout included calisthenics, push-ups, sit-ups, chin-ups, and a run of four miles on average. Sometimes we ran as a company, but more often as platoons or squads.

These were the runs that I liked best, getting away from the streetlights on post and jogging along the back roads around Fort Benning. Running in silence. Alone with our thoughts. Yet together as a unit. I reveled in the sharp, metered precision of it—each man keeping stride with the group by the reverberating sound of the others' footfalls.

Normally we would have been singing cadence, the time-honored tradition that made it easier to stay in step while running in a group, though we did it more out of habit than necessity. These silent runs, however, gave a stronger feeling of our being one body, more like parts of a living organism than a team of individuals. As much as it frustrated me sometimes, I really appreciated the sense of order and esprit de corps that existed among this elite group of warriors.

We were keeping a strong seven-minute pace, much faster than the Army standard of eight minutes per mile, but not particularly difficult for most of us. Privates with orange reflective vests and flashlights ran thirty meters ahead of the platoon and also to the rear, ready to alert any oncoming traffic to proceed slowly. Whenever a vehicle did go by, its headlights threw undulating shadows throughout the formation and illuminated a curl of condensed breath rising above us like a collective halo, giving the scene a surreal look.

Civilians would sometimes wonder aloud why we didn't fit their notion of what a Ranger should look like, which apparently bore some resemblance to an NFL linebacker. In reality, most of the men in the unit were built like long-distance runners or swimmers. In this outfit, agility was preferred to size, and endurance prized over brute strength. More than once on a long road march, I'd had to take over a machine gun from one of the larger guys in the platoon when he began dropping back. Being big simply meant that you had more to lug around.

Sometimes people would ask why we exercised so much. The simple answer was that we never got in good enough shape to quit. Fitness is like that, as are many areas of life.

This same principle certainly applied to my spiritual life.

Unfortunately, I had neglected to keep a regular quiet time of reading my Bible and praying. Not surprisingly, my faith had become flabby and out of shape. I tried to rationalize that since I'd been a Christian for a long time, God knew that I belonged to Him and wouldn't mind not hearing from me *every* day. The result, however, was that I didn't get to hear from *Him*, which left me more vulnerable to spiritual compromise.

My relationship with Christ never grew at a steady rate. I experienced long stretches where I didn't feel His presence or power in my life because of having fallen into some sin. Other times I just allowed myself to be buried under the weight of necessity to such an extent that it wasn't possible to give God the first and best part of me.

And then there were those times when God felt close enough to touch.

My spiritual life developed kind of like the rings on a tree, with spurts of rapid growth and nourishment interspersed with long winters of hibernation. Intellectually, I knew it was a bad idea to wander away from God's daily presence, but as usual, the difficulty wasn't in the knowing—it was in the *doing*.

Today's run was a bit longer than usual, around seven miles. We followed the road that skirted the edge of the airfield and the Chattahoochee River. It was a Monday, and I'd been looking forward to getting back to work. My roommate, Mike, had been getting on my nerves a little, like all friends do from time to time. Jennifer was out of town, so I had planned to zone out in front of the TV on Sunday afternoon, but Mike had wanted to talk. He liked to get into deep philosophical discussions at every opportunity, exploring the great questions of life until all hours of the night. Mike was eleven years my senior and extremely intelligent, so I normally found our conversations engaging. But this weekend I'd just wanted to hibernate and couldn't seem to get that across to Mike. I valued Mike as a generous and devoted friend, but his occasional inability to read my mood sometimes grated on me.

At one point I got a little frustrated and blurted out, "Mike, if you had yourself a girlfriend, you might have something better to do than pester me all the time." That hit a nerve with him, and he got up and left the room, looking a little hurt. I knew the comment was uncalled-for but rationalized that he had had it coming. Mike wanted a girlfriend, but as with many guys, finding one wasn't so easy for him. For me dating was as natural as breathing, and our differing perspectives had often been a major point of contention between us. Mike would argue that it wasn't healthy for me to have to *always* have a girlfriend, because it stifled my relationships with other friends. I'd declare that he was just jealous.

Anyway, this run was just what I needed. Lieutenant McDaniel, our platoon leader (PL), stayed at the front of the formation, setting the pace for the entire group. He was in great shape and liked to push us. Since running was my strong suit, I enjoyed the challenge. For a few in the platoon, however, running at a normal pace was challenge enough. It was these men who showed the first signs of trouble as we approached the final mile of the run. By that point, most of us were thankful that we weren't calling cadence and could focus our energies on other things—like keeping up with the platoon leader and breathing!

A moderately steep hill rose for about a quarter mile from the airfield up to the barracks, and it was clear as the formation approached that the PL had no intention of slowing down. We began exchanging breathless glances, preparing ourselves mentally to take the incline. By the time we were halfway up, however, it was starting to hurt. The PL was keeping his pace steady, but we were beginning to spread out. The rhythm of our shoes on the pavement began to disintegrate as a few men got out of step. This caused the runners behind them to break stride to avoid stepping on their heels.

We continued to labor up the hill, and two men began to fall out of the formation completely. The PL kept running, and Sergeant Kelly, who was struggling as hard as any of us, shouted, "Tighten it up, ladies!" His orders, however, met with little success. The more our platoon spread out, the more the volume and pitch of his commands rose. He berated the two who were now twenty yards or more behind the formation, yelling, "Move it, men! Around here we play catch-up, not wait-up!"

It was no use. The men who had fallen out simply didn't have enough left to make it back into place, even once we reached the top of the hill. The two fallouts lumbered along, breathing in great gasps until one of them stopped completely and began retching on the side of the road.

Sergeant Kelly had had enough. He cursed, then turned to the platoon and said simply, "Go get 'em, men."

A collective groan arose from our ranks. Squad leaders quickly began calling out the names of their strongest runners as Lieutenant McDaniel did a U-turn and headed back to get the stragglers.

"Howle! Bickford! Steadman! Hill!" called the First Squad leader.

Sergeant Friar added, "Holton! Reynolds! Smith! Perdue!"

The eight of us broke ranks and ran back to the beleaguered fallouts. We each grabbed an arm or leg and hoisted the panting men onto our shoulders, then struggled toward the formation, which had mercifully slowed so that we could catch up.

Those of us doing the carrying weren't exactly happy about it. As we huffed and puffed under the added weight of our companions, some not-so-nice assertions were offered up about them, and none of us made much of an effort to ensure that they had a comfortable ride. I was particularly miffed because it was obvious that Sheldon, the man I was helping to carry, had been out drinking the night before, which had no doubt contributed to his difficulties this morning. I didn't appreciate having to literally carry his weight just because he hadn't been responsible enough to get to bed at a decent hour.

"Let's dump him in the ditch and leave him," spat Reynolds, only half joking.

"Good idea," I puffed.

"I get his shoes," added Perdue, playing along.

Sheldon looked down at us and said, "Hey! It's not... Ow!" He let out a tirade of profanity at having received a shoulder in the kidney.

It wasn't long before the men being carried had had enough. "OK, OK! Put me down!" Sheldon screeched. We were only too glad to comply, then hurried to catch back up with the body of the formation.

As we rounded the corner and came within sight of the company area, the platoon surged ahead, almost as if carried by a wave of energy created by the presence of the chow hall. Like horses headed for the stable, we all felt a shot of adrenaline upon seeing the finish line. We ran expectantly, listening for the platoon leader to call back over his shoulder the command that would signal the end of the run: "Quick time, march!"

But the command didn't come.

The PL continued running right past the company area, keeping the same steady pace that we'd held for most of the run. The energy that I'd been feeling a moment earlier faded as we passed the chow hall and continued down the street. It was obvious that the other men felt the same way I did, but to their credit, no one fell out, though all of us wanted to. Now collectively short of breath, we resigned ourselves to following the platoon leader down the block and around the corner.

The PL ran us just once more around the block that housed the regiment, though it seemed like miles, before finally calling a halt. Then, Sergeant First Class Kelly marched the panting and steaming platoon from the street onto the PT field across from our barracks, calling, "Left; left; left, right!" at intervals to keep us in step.

"Platoon, halt!" We stopped as one.

"Left, face!" The platoon turned to face him. "Open ranks, march!" We spread out to the left of the squad leaders, who were standing at the head of each column. Every man spread his arms out to the sides at shoulder level to measure the correct distance from the man on either side.

Sergeant Kelly continued to bark out commands in quick, practiced succession. "Arms downward, move! Left, face! Open ranks, march! Arms downward, move! Right, face!" We followed his commands until each man in the platoon had approximately eight feet of space in which to move. Then Sergeant First Class Kelly completed the maneuver with a final, simple command.

"Rest!"

A relieved "Hooah!" rippled through the platoon. This was just the sort of daily drill and ceremony that was so much a part of our lives that none of us thought twice about how to do it. If PT was the Ranger equivalent of daily devotionals, drill and ceremony was our form of liturgy.

"Stretch out, men!"

We did so, and I thought about how difficult the last unexpected half mile of the run had been. I was convinced that had we been expecting to go seven and a half miles, no one would have been bothered by that last half mile. But since our minds were set on running seven miles and stopping as usual in front of the chow hall, when our PL kept going, our expectations were dashed. The energy drained out of us as if someone had pulled a plug. It was clear that the first seven miles were intended to strengthen our bodies, and the extra half mile was to strengthen our minds. Our platoon leader clearly understood that a strong body is useless if inhabited by a weak mind, and vice versa. And both need daily exercise.

After we had cooled off from the run, we all paired up with a buddy and ran through our standard regimen of push-ups and sit-ups. Then we completed a set of flutter kicks as a platoon, steam rising from our bodies as we counted in unison.

With that, Sergeant Kelly got up and barked, "On your feet!"

Once we had recovered and again closed ranks into a standard formation, Sergeant Kelly called out the Weapons Squad leader.

"Sergeant Smith, come and lead us in the Ranger Creed."

The Ranger Creed was the closest thing to Scripture that some Rangers ever knew. Its six stanzas embodied the Ranger spirit, and we all had learned in RIP to recite them from memory. Sergeant Smith had been at the battalion longer than anyone in our platoon, and he felt particularly passionate about the values expressed in the creed. It was especially inspiring to recite the creed with him, since he did it with a gusto that made it clear that he believed every word. I had thought more than once that if Christians would quote Scripture with the same passion that Smitty brought to the Ranger Creed, our churches would never want for new members.

Sergeant Smith ran to the front of the formation and began, adding testosterone-laced emphasis to the words as he spoke.

"The first stanza of the Ranger Creed! Repeat after me!

"Recognizing that I volunteered as a Ranger, fully know-ing the hazards of my chosen profession, I will always endeavor to uphold the prestige, honor, and high esprit de corps of my Ranger regiment."

We echoed the stanza back to him, and he moved on to the next.

"Acknowledging the fact that a Ranger is a more elite sol-dier who arrives at the cutting edge of battle by land, sea, or air, I accept the fact that as a Ranger my country expects me to move farther, faster and fight harder than any other soldier."

I repeated the stanzas in unison with the platoon and contem-plated the true meaning of the words. At the same time, strong spiritual parallels attached themselves in my mind to each verse as it left my lips. I felt that the pride of being an elite soldier was inextricably linked to the concept of being set apart by God, called out of the ranks of ordinary soldiers, and given a more difficult assignment to fulfill for Him.

"Never shall I fail my comrades. I will always keep myself mentally alert, physically strong, and morally straight, and I will shoulder more than my share of the task whatever it may be, one hundred percent and then some."

And the reward for accepting the call to this mission was that we'd get the privilege of living in the company of others who held a similar call. We'd been allowed to enter a brotherhood of men who shared a bond that most people could never understand. It was a brotherhood of shared belief, shared hardship, and shared purpose.

"Gallantly will I show the world that I am a specially selected and well trained soldier. My courtesy to superior officers, neatness of dress, and care of equipment shall set the example for others to follow."

What an honor it was to belong to a group whose members pledged to cultivate an environment where men felt compelled not to be simply good, but *better*. This was one of the same reasons that I appreciated belonging to a group of believers—the example that we strove to set was as much for one another as it was for those who looked to us for answers.

Sergeant Smith was really getting into it now. It crossed my mind that he'd make a dynamite motivational speaker. His enthusiasm was infectious, and the soldiers in our platoon were sounding off at the top of their lungs as they continued to follow his lead.

"Energetically will I meet the enemies of my country. I shall defeat them on the field of battle for I am better trained and will fight with all my might. Surrender is not a Ranger word. I will never leave a fallen comrade to fall into the hands of the enemy and under no circumstances will I ever embarrass my country.

"Readily will I display the intestinal fortitude required to fight on to the Ranger objective and complete the mission, though I be the lone survivor."

Rangers never quit, on each other or on themselves. If I didn't get anything else out of my time at regiment, this mind-set was enough to make it worthwhile.

Sergeant Smith's voice rose as he concluded, "Rangers, lead the way!"

The sound of our voices echoed his and rattled the windows of the barracks in front of us.

RANGERS NEVER QUIT, ON EACH OTHER OR ON THEMSELVES.

Smitty returned to his place in the formation and Sergeant First Class Kelly stepped up again. "OK, men. Get cleaned up and go to chow. Next formation at 0900. Fall out!"

"Hooah!"

Five minutes later I was signing my name on the chow hall register, all that was required for an enlisted man to dine there. I grabbed a tray and sidled up to the food counter, where the cooks were doling out French toast, bacon, eggs, and the ubiquitous biscuits and gravy. Good food was one of the perks of being a Ranger. Our chow hall was allotted 50 percent more money per man than a regular Army unit, which gave us little to complain about as far as the quality or quantity of the food we were served.

I decided to wait while the cook prepared an omelette. While I was waiting, Sheldon walked up and stopped beside me with his meal tray already containing a full plate of biscuits and gravy. He was still wearing his sweaty PT uniform, as was I. He and I had arrived at the battalion within months of each other, and though we had never hung around together off duty, we'd been on enough missions together to enjoy an easy familiarity. It was the sort of bond common to all men who have shared miserable circumstances. Sheldon was known for his easygoing manner, if not for his intellect. It was a reputation that he didn't seem to mind, however.

"Hey, Holton," he said. "Sorry you had to carry me this morning. I really shoulda gotten more sleep last night."

"You're right about that. Maybe it also had something to do with the keg you swallowed," I answered matter-of-factly.

"Well, I guess I owe you one." His voice took on a tinge of sarcasm in reaction to my tone. "Unless you count the time I carried you to the exfil chopper on that raid we did at Fort Chaffee last year."

Touché. I'd forgotten about that. Perhaps I'd been too harsh. I turned to him and said, "Hey, you're right. I know you'd do the same for me. Tell you what, buy my breakfast and we'll call it even."

Sheldon grinned and rolled his eyes as he headed off for the drink machines. "OK, whatever."

I finished filling my tray with food and then headed for an empty table in the corner of the chow hall. After saying grace, I dug into the pile of steaming breakfast food. I felt bad for having been so harsh toward Sheldon. The hill had been tough on all of us, even the good runners. Sheldon was a big guy, definitely Clydesdale class, when it came to running. He probably would have had trouble even if he'd been fully rested. And it wasn't like he hadn't given it his best effort, regardless of his choices the night before.

I had conveniently forgotten about my own failing on the mission at the Joint Readiness Training Center at Fort Chaffee, Arkansas. It was a fast-rope mission into a mock prison camp where I had been a little too audacious and was "killed" by an observer/controller who was acting as a referee. Sheldon had single-handedly carried me and my gear at least two hundred meters to the Chinook helicopter that was our ride home.

But even if he hadn't, it wasn't fair for me to rub his nose in his own failings now.

Come to think of it, I had been doing the same thing to Mike. Most of the girls in our singles group at church were college students, in their late teens and early twenties, and most of them preferred to date someone close to their own age. Guys like Mike who were "confirmed bachelors" had the odds stacked against them at the outset, so it was no wonder they got fewer dates than I did. It certainly wasn't right for me to put Mike down for it, any more than it would be for me to ostracize a divorced single. I hadn't thought about it before, but wasn't I displaying a selfish unwillingness to consider the issues Mike was dealing with, contrary to the Bible's admonition to "carry each other's burdens"?

When the fifth stanza of the Ranger Creed promises, "I will never leave a fallen comrade," it doesn't qualify the statement with "unless it's his own fault." The front line is never the place to ask the wounded soldier *why* it happened. The only thing that matters at the time is safeguarding the wounded man and getting him treated. In the church, however, we often have the tendency to point the finger at someone right away. Shouldn't soldiers in God's army be at least as willing to stick by each other when times get tough, regardless of who's at fault?

By unearthing my own motives in this situation, I was getting a glimpse of why people who judge Christianity by the actions of its followers might sometimes find themselves turned off by believers' self-righteous, superior attitudes. It made me wince to think about it. How many souls would spend eternity apart from God because of a callous attitude or thoughtless word?

After all, I thought, *isn't it the stragglers who most need patience and understanding? Why do we Christians sometimes have a tendency to shoot our wounded?*

The answer was immediately clear to me: *Because it is the easy way out.* Bearing my brother's burden doubles my workload. It's easy to become resentful of the injured one. But this morning's conversation with Sheldon reminded me that sometimes the injured one is me.

In thinking back to our run that morning, remembering what a brain workout that extra half mile was, I could suddenly see the parallel: Carrying my own weight in life is good for my mind, but shouldering the weight of another is good for my soul.

12

OPERATION JUST CAUSE

God and the soldier, we adore
In time of danger, not before.
The danger past, and all things righted
God is forgotten, the soldier slighted.

UNKNOWN

A man is immortal until God is finished with him.

JIM ELLIOT

20 DECEMBER 1989, 0100, H-HOUR

Two seconds of silence. Falling.

Then the bone-jarring opening shock of the parachute knocking the wind out of me. I decelerated from 150 knots to a virtual standstill in another two seconds. The sounds returned: the roar of the C-130 disappearing into the black velvet night, the billowing chute above. Though it surely wasn't silent in those four seconds after I exited the aircraft, it had seemed that way on every one of the thirty-four jumps I'd made. It's something I never got used to.

Rio Hato Airfield was an unusual airport. The laminated map

in my pocket showed its single runway lying north to south, a quarter mile off the Atlantic Ocean. The weird thing about it is that the Pan-American Highway cuts right through the middle of the airfield, going east-west. Every time they want to land a plane, they have to stop traffic on the two-lane highway to do so. Why the road wasn't diverted around the airfield is a complete mystery. Forty miles to the north, more of our Ranger brethren were dropping on top of Torrijos-Tocumen International Airport in Panama City. Rio Hato's tactical significance lay in the fact that it housed two companies of Panamanian special forces, an officers training academy, and a beach house that belonged to Manuel Noriega.

It was as dark as the inside of a cow. Swinging in my parachute harness, I searched quickly for something recognizable on the ground, but could see only a few pinpoints of light. I suddenly realized that I was facing away from the airfield and began to look frantically over each shoulder, aware that in about ten seconds I'd be too low to see anything. I still wasn't able to discern anything that jibed with the map we had spent hours memorizing.

Then I saw buildings below me.

Where were there buildings on the map?

I recalled some on the leading edge of the drop zone, which would have meant that I was south of the highway that traverses the airfield. It didn't even occur to me that if this were the case, many of the jumpers ahead of me had most likely landed in the ocean. I became aware of a snapping above my head—the sound wasn't unfamiliar, yet I couldn't quite place it. I wondered if my chute had blown a panel, but a quick check showed it to be intact.

Time's up. I still don't know where I am.

I felt the ground coming up to meet me. It's hard to explain, but

I couldn't see it or hear it; I just felt it. Normally the rucksack hanging at my waist would have been released to drop fifteen feet below me on the lowering line attached to my harness. I intentionally didn't lower it this time, however, increasing the chances of breaking a bone upon landing but making it possible to get moving quicker by keeping everything on my person.

The instant before my boots impacted with the ground at seventeen feet per second—the equivalent of jumping fully encumbered from a twelve-foot platform—I realized what the snapping sounds were in my chute.

Bullets.

Aimed at me.

I performed an awkward parachute landing fall, bruising my legs on the rucksack, and I rolled over on my back just in time to see two tracers perforate my parachute as it slowly deflated above me. As the bullets whizzed by two feet over my head, I heard the same snapping sound I remembered from the live-fire range. The sound of the bullet going by makes a *snap! snap!* followed closely by a more distant *pop! pop!* of the gun doing the shooting.

Great. I'm being shot at.

My landing put me in a low spot overgrown with five-foot-tall grass. Good thing. If I'd landed in the open, those rounds might have found me. I lay still, sweating, listening for the sound of the enemy approaching, hearing nothing but my own heartbeat.

After about ten seconds, I realized that my rifle/grenade launcher was still zipped in its case at my side. For all practical purposes, I was unarmed and defenseless until I could get out of the harness and get to my weapon. It probably took me thirty seconds to do this, but it seemed like an hour. Adrenaline was running so thick in my veins that I found myself shivering involuntarily, like I had just drunk a case of Mountain Dew. I felt like I was moving in slow motion.

Tracers were arcing up into the sky over the airfield. The Panamanians were shooting at the other planes still dropping their jumpers. Some of the planes were dropping chaff flares to confuse any heat-seeking missiles that might be launched. I could see jumpers silhouetted in their light. Later I heard that in one plane, a round came through the skin of the aircraft and hit a man before he could get out the door. His comrades had to quickly unhook and go around him, then hook back up before jumping. Reportedly, the wounded soldier was more upset about not getting to jump with his buddies than he was about being shot. He survived.

Weapon in hand, I crawled toward the sound of the guns and immediately came upon a road. A lone thatch hut faced me on the other side. Whoever had been shooting at me had stopped.

Where are the other six hundred guys who jumped with me?

I could see no one and suddenly felt incredibly alone. The first things to be done were to hook up with another Ranger and get my bearings. By heading north, it seemed like I'd probably run into the Pan-American Highway, and from there I'd be able to find my assembly area halfway up the south side of the airfield.

I took a deep breath and charged across the road, weapon trained on the thatch hut. It was empty. It was then that I noticed several similar huts spaced evenly down the road. The map hadn't shown any villages, so finding this one only confused me further as to my whereabouts. I crouched down by the corner of the hut, thinking about what useless cover it would make if whoever was shooting decided to start up again.

The hut was at the intersection of two narrow dirt roads. Across from me, a parachute fluttered from a telephone pole. Following it with my eyes, I finally picked out another Ranger furiously packing up his gear at the base of it, oblivious to my presence. I didn't recognize him.

"Bulldog! Bulldog!" I called out, trying to shout in a whisper our agreed-upon running password. He didn't respond, so I decided to cross over to him. A quick check up the road showed it to be deserted. As soon as I charged out into the street, however, *snap! snap! snap!* White tracers went zipping by at kneecap level. I hit the brakes and ran back to the thatch hut. The rounds had come from about a block away, off to my right. Forgetting about the Ranger across from me, I sent a few rounds back at whoever was shooting, and then stopped abruptly, worried that the sound of my firing would draw fire from others. I was also worried about shooting one of our own guys.

After moving west and clearing two more thatch huts, I still had no idea where I was. Some serious shooting was going on to my south. Then I heard the password whispered behind me. It was Sergeant Wentland from First Platoon.

"Is the highway that way?" I asked, pointing north.

"Nope," he said, "it's over there," motioning toward the sound of the shooting.

Sheesh. I wonder how far north I would have gone before figuring that out? I shrugged. "All right then, let's go to the guns."

We moved out south, skirting as quietly as possible through people's yards, climbing wire fences, dashing across side streets. Along the way I found Bohannon, my new private. Other than somehow landing on his nose, he was all right. I pulled his bleeding face close to mine. "Do exactly what I do and you'll be fine."

Bohannon gulped. "Roger, Specialist."

I remembered Specialist Hill giving the same command on my first training mission with the unit more than two years earlier. Those words had been very reassuring to me. I hoped that my voice sounded as confident as his had. Knowing that I was responsible for Private Bohannon took the edge off my own fear. It also helped not to be running around the battlefield alone anymore.

By then, we were hearing "Bulldog!" whispered everywhere. Men were starting to team up and get organized. We linked up with Specialist Shelley, who carried a SAW for Second Squad, and soon after, the four of us came upon the Pan-American Highway. In the mission brief, it had been emphasized that the road across the airfield was to be kept free of traffic at all costs. Upon reaching the roadway, we saw a driverless tanker truck with a revolving yellow light on its roof blocking the road from the east at the edge of the airfield. I hoped that no one would get the bright idea to shoot that truck and make it explode.

> KNOWING THAT I WAS RESPONSIBLE FOR PRIVATE BOHANNON TOOK THE EDGE OFF MY OWN FEAR.

Shots rang out sporadically from all directions. At this point I was more worried about being shot by a Ranger than an enemy soldier. I could see fire teams moving in wedge formations across the runway. The four of us were lying prone by the edge of the highway, along with about ten other soldiers.

In the middle of the road in front of us stood Command Sergeant Major Leon-Guerrero, the regimental CSM. A short, muscular man, he looked oblivious to the bullets flying this way and that. "Come on, men!" He gestured for us to get up. "Move out!" The sight of him was incredibly motivating.

I noticed a red flashing radio tower on the other side of the air-field, to the southwest. That had to be Objective Dog, our platoon's first target. We were supposed to blow that tower. Inspired by CSM Guerrero, Shelley, Bohannon, and I headed off toward the flashing beacon at a trot. We crossed the highway and didn't get fifty yards before hearing a surge of fire behind us. Turning, we saw a white four-door compact car come speeding out onto the highway, attempting to cross the airfield. People on either side of the high-way were shooting at it. We turned and started to fire at it also, but then realized that we were in a bad position, shooting back toward Rangers who were shooting in our direction. We stopped firing momentarily and hugged the airfield tarmac, as friendly fire zipped over our heads. The car screeched to a halt, and someone got out of the driver's side and opened the rear door before our bullets hit home. The driver toppled into the backseat.

Cautiously, Rangers approached the fallen driver, who was obviously dead and, now obviously, a woman.

Someone turned her over. She was lying on a rocket-propelled grenade launcher. I had been worried that we had shot a noncom-batant for a second, but no longer. She was the first enemy soldier I saw in the invasion. Her lower jaw was missing.

But we didn't have time to dwell on it. I reminded myself to stay focused on the mission.

I grabbed Bohannon and turned again toward our objective.

We moved back toward Objective Dog, our platoon's assembly point. Halfway there, a friendly machine gun opened up on Dog, signaling that the assault had already begun. We picked up the pace, and upon reaching the objective, met up with about ten others from

Second Platoon. Sergeant Friar wasn't among them. The reality that he may have become a casualty put a knot in my gut.

The platoon was in the middle of clearing the buildings at the objective. We dropped our rucksacks and joined them. Most of the buildings turned out to be empty, though we found a sizable cache of weapons in one of them. At one point we started taking fire from the line of trees behind the buildings. I dove to the ground beside a large concrete sign near me. The sign had a gaudy painting identifying the military school housed here. It provided no real protection from the hostile fire, but it was the only semblance of cover around. My fellow team leader, Tom Stoner, flopped down on the other side of the sign and looked around the corner at me, grinning.

"Pretty fun, huh?" he quipped.

I shot him a look that said, *Yeah, right.*

I was holding a Light Antitank Weapon (LAW) that I had picked up off the ground while crossing the airfield. A one-lane paved road lay behind us. Then someone shouted, "There's a truck coming down the road!" Stoner and I looked at each other for an instant, and then he grabbed the LAW out of my hands and charged out into the road with no one covering him.

"Hey!" I yelled, running after him. "Get back here!"

Stoner stopped in the middle of the road, with the truck bearing down on him. Before he could arm the LAW, someone else hit it broadside with one and flipped it into the ditch. Stoner was truly disappointed that he didn't get to shoot the truck. He dropped the LAW to the pavement and unleashed a string of curses. He was beginning to scare me. Later I realized that Stoner knew better than any of us, perhaps, what a historic moment we were in, and he simply wanted to play an important part in it.

We then turned our attention to the next objective, which was the military academy barracks, code-named Objective Silver. Sergeant First Class Kelly gave the order to flank around to approach the barracks from the side, where there were the fewest windows. He was a veteran of Grenada in 1983, and I thought about how he had just earned his second combat jump star, a rare accomplishment. A foul-tempered person on a good day, he was nevertheless a very good soldier. We hadn't always gotten along, but I was glad to have him here leading us now.

Sergeant First Class Kelly sent five men from First Squad up to the school compound to make sure that it was empty, as intel had said it would be. The cadets were supposed to be home for Christmas. The rest of us waited in the woods.

A call came over on the radio from Sergeant Smith, First Squad leader. They had come upon three unoccupied vehicles and heard voices inside the school. SFC Kelly spat and then turned to me. "Holton, you speak Spanish, right?"

"I, well, uh…"

"Good. Get up there and get those zoomies to surrender." *Zoomies* was a mildly derogatory term used to refer to members of a country's air force.

"Roger that, Sergeant."

I was quickly gaining an aversion to open spaces. As I left the relative safety of the woods and moved toward the corner of the school building where First Platoon was waiting, I thought about my three years of high school Spanish. I wished my teachers had spent a little more time teaching us how to say things like, "Come out with your hands up!"

Boom! Boom!

Two explosions rocked the building in front of me. I hit the dirt.

13

THE BOTTOM LINE

To save your world you asked this man to die;
Would this man, could he see you now, ask why?

W. H. AUDEN, "EPITAPH FOR AN UNKNOWN SOLDIER"

"The waves of death swirled about me; the torrents of destruction overwhelmed me.
The cords of the grave coiled around me; the snares of death confronted me.
In my distress I called to the LORD; I called out to my God.
From his temple he heard my voice; my cry came to his ears."

2 SAMUEL 22:5–7

"Move it, Holton!" First Squad leader called. I ran up to the building. Three cars were parked in front of it; one of them was a gleaming new Nissan Sentra. It seemed out of place in what was, for the most part, a third world country. Five Rangers waited in the murky shadows, stacked up under a portico at the front of the horseshoe-shaped building. They were peering around the corner into a courtyard with several doors facing into it.

"What was that?" I asked, out of breath.

"Someone ran out of that door there," Smith answered, pointing into the courtyard in front of us. "He went for that breezeway at the back. Harbison sent a couple of high explosive rounds after him."

Our lieutenant came on the radio. "Hurry up! Keep clearing! The buildings are empty!"

I looked around the corner as Smith informed him again that they were indeed *not* empty. Smoke curled from a grapefruit-sized hole in the back wall of the building. I racked my brain for the right words in Spanish to diffuse the situation, but failed. All I could manage was *"Venga aca!"* (Come here!) and *"No muerto!"* (No die!). I tried this three times, with no success.

"No one is coming out," Smith whispered into his mike.

Sergeant First Class Kelly's reply crackled back.

"OK, go in hot."

We moved in single file around to the first door. It was slightly open. Smith pulled the pin on a grenade, flipped the spoon away, and a second later lobbed it upward in the door toward the ceiling.

"Frag out!"

I plugged my ears. Seconds later, windows shattered everywhere, including the louvered windows high above our heads, and glass rained down on us.

Chaos.

Smith and Harbison burst into the room spraying bullets, immediately followed by high-pitched voices calling in Spanish, *"No mas! No mas!"* Panamanian soldiers had been hiding under their bunks. Now eight of them were standing with their hands in the air. All of them were injured, either from the grenade or the subsequent shooting. The sight of a mattress on fire registered in my brain as I passed the room.

Sonnenschein kicked in the door to the next room. Seeing immediately how crowded it was with furniture, he remained outside and did not throw the grenade that was in his hand. Looking over the sights of my weapon, I saw that the room was very large and full of bunk beds. From under each bed there was a pair of hands sticking up, and muffled voices yelling surrender. The lights were not working. The guy under the bunk closest to the door was holding a flashlight, however, so I stepped in and grabbed it from his trembling hands. He looked to be about my age. I swept the room with the light, and it was obvious that the students of this military school had not gone home for Christmas. This room had at least forty students in it.

I started calling the cadets out of the room. "Get up! Get up! *Mueve! Mueve!*"

We didn't have enough Rangers at the objective to handle the Panamanian defense forces (PDF) coming out of the building. Things were getting hairy. I got on the radio, shouting, "Get more people up here! We need help!" I moved quickly on to the next doorway, now joined by Stoner. By this time, First Squad had all of the occupants of the first room outside, lined up against the wall. They were bleeding all over the concrete and broken glass. The rest of the students were being arranged facedown in the grassy courtyard.

There were two doors to the next room that Stoner and I encountered, situated right next to each other for some reason. He and I decided to kick them open on the count of three. When we did, his door opened easily, but mine felt like someone was leaning on it. Aiming downward, I fired a three round burst into the door. It still wouldn't open. My ears were ringing. I moved around to Stoner's door. It was another big room, with more hands sprouting from under bunks. I realized that we had to do something with these guys, so I waded into the room shouting at the men to get up and out into the courtyard. They hesitated, so I fired another round into the ceiling. That got them moving. I saw the reason why my door wouldn't open—there was a bunk bed pushed up against it. A teenage cadet emerged from under that bunk. It was a miracle that my three-round burst into the door didn't hit him.

Sergeant First Class Kelly had heard the firing and thought we were in trouble, so he sent the entire platoon. It was just as well, though, because the six of us were now greatly outnumbered by military cadets frantic to surrender.

Everyone was yelling at once.

The students filed out of the large room, hands in the air, while Stoner and I kept them covered with our M-16s. I shone the flashlight up at their hands, looking for anyone who might possibly have a knife or grenade. I saw a glint of metal in one cadet's hand and almost pulled the trigger on him. I began yelling, *"En la mano!"* (In your hand!). He opened his hand to reveal a fancy wristwatch. I eased the pressure on my trigger finger and told him angrily, "You just almost died for that watch!" He gave me a scared, quizzical look.

I realized that my limited Spanish was not going to help us much, so I asked if any of the cadets spoke English. Two of them did. I pulled them aside and asked, "Are there any others in this building?" They both nodded and said that there were also some who had fled out the back into the jungle. One of them said, "We've been waiting for you to come." He sounded relieved. It struck me that I had absolutely no animosity toward these men. They were younger than my nineteen years and plainly scared out of their wits. An ID card from one of the students was lying on the ground at my feet. I picked it up and put it in my pocket.

"OK, here's what we're going to do," I told them. "You two come with us out back and call to your amigos. Tell them to surrender or die. We'll be right behind you."

Others searched the rest of the building and tended to the prisoners, while Stoner and I moved cautiously through the breezeway, following the two cadets, who were shouting in Spanish. As we emerged at the rear of the building, we could see a basketball court, the far side of which dropped off into the jungle. Several sets of raised hands appeared from there. I shone the flashlight at them. A voice inside my head reminded me that the flashlight in my hand made me a great target. I berated myself silently and threw the flashlight into the bushes.

Then, off to our left, I heard the clatter of a weapon on pavement. Jumpy, I instinctively swung my weapon in that direction and dropped to a crouch. There was an AK-47 lying on the basketball court. A PDF officer appeared out of the jungle, hands held high. Staff Sergeant Friar and Sergeant Sonnenschein appeared around the side of the building on my left with their weapons trained on him. The officer was surrendering to them. Stoner began moving our prisoners back to the courtyard, and I moved to retrieve the AK-47.

> I WAS REALLY ANGRY WITH MYSELF—IT WAS THE KIND OF MISTAKE THAT COULD HAVE GOTTEN ME KILLED.

I was glad to see that Staff Sergeant Friar had made it. He began searching the prisoner when I suddenly wondered if the PDF officer hadn't just tried to shoot me. I'd been holding that stupid flashlight, and the officer probably decided to surrender only when his weapon jammed. I was really angry with myself for that tactical lapse of judgment. It was the kind of mistake that could have easily gotten me killed.

Staff Sergeant Friar searched the prisoner, and Sonnenschein covered him with his M-16. I slung the discarded AK-47 over my shoulder and then pulled security in the direction of the jungle. Then Friar found a set of car keys.

"I'll bet those go to that Nissan out front," I remarked. "It's nicer than my car."

Staff Sergeant Friar tossed them to me. "Go check. We may need to commandeer it."

"Roger, Sergeant." I turned and jogged back toward the front of the building, rounding the corner just in time to see Sergeant Smith smash the driver's window out of the Nissan with his rifle butt. Apparently he had the same idea we did. When I walked up and handed him the keys, he let out a groan.

A prisoner of war collection point was set up about a third of a mile from the school. We eventually collected one hundred and sixty-seven prisoners from the supposedly empty barracks. We spent the next several hours shuttling them in groups of twenty-five, walking single file to the collection point. During this time I became acutely aware of how exhausted I was.

Sergeant First Class Kelly had warned us that as soon as the adrenaline started to wear off, we'd be more tired than ever before in our lives. He was right. It was all I could do to keep walking, leading our groups of POWs.

On the way back from one of the seven trips made to the collection point, I passed a rucksack lying next to the road, still attached to a parachute and its harness. I reached in and grabbed the two-quart canteen of water that was standard equipment in every Ranger rucksack. Seconds later, the canteen was empty. I couldn't remember ever being so thirsty. A little dog went skittering by, startling me. I instinctively hit the dirt, then got back up quickly, embarrassed.

It was almost 0500 by the time we got the POWs taken care of, and it was starting to get light. Only one of those injured by the first fragmentation grenade that we threw was in serious condition. We heard later that he suffered some internal bleeding.

Staff Sergeant Friar marked up the Nissan with orange marker panels to identify it as friendly, and had me drive him to the battalion command post (CP) and casualty collection point to report our findings to the commander. While they were meeting, I stood around outside talking with some of the other Rangers. Apparently the invasion had gone well, and it seemed that, except for some small pockets of resistance, the airfield was secure.

While we were talking, two jeeps came roaring into the CP with some of our wounded on them. We ran over to help get them into the aid station. One man had both legs missing and was trembling in extreme pain. Another had been shot in the neck and was so covered in blood that he was almost unrecognizable. He was clearly dead. People were running in all directions as I picked up one end of the stretcher containing our fallen comrade, and with the help of another Ranger, carried him into the aid station. There were several other casualties in the makeshift triage, most of them only slightly wounded.

We set the dead Ranger down in the corner and stepped back outside. I was disturbed by what I'd just seen. Until now the only casualties that I had encountered were enemy. I was prepared for that; it's what was supposed to happen. But now I'd been reminded that our side bleeds, too, and it left me shaken.

I saw Captain Bloomstrom, the Third Battalion chaplain, step out of the triage unit and walk toward me. He was a good friend and confidant. I'd had dinner with him and his wife, and he had attended some of the choir musicals put on by my church back at Fort Benning.

He had jumped into Rio Hato armed only with a Bible. I went over to meet him, giving him a pained smile. He did not smile back.

"Do you know who that was?" he asked.

"Who what was, sir?"

"The guy you just carried in."

I shrugged. "Somebody from Second Bat, I think."

He lifted his hand and opened it for me to see. He was holding a set of dog tags, covered in blood.

LEAR, PHILIP S

My breath caught as I stared at the name in disbelief. Time slowed to a crawl.

"I'm sorry, Chuck. You knew him, didn't you?"

Images of Lear and me in Ranger school flooded my memory. I recalled standing with him during the impromptu worship service that the chaplain had given before we boarded the aircraft for this mission and his confident grin as I shook his hand before we jumped, less than seven hours ago. Could he have been the same Ranger lying blood-soaked on that stretcher? *No! This can't be!*

I sat down on the curb in shock. Suddenly I felt older, much older.

"It could have been any one of us. We all volunteered for this," the chaplain said.

I swallowed hard. "You're right, sir. We knew what we were getting into. He was my Ranger buddy in Ranger school."

Just then Staff Sergeant Friar appeared. He was done with his meeting and began walking toward the vehicle, oblivious to what had just happened.

"Holton! Let's move."

"Are you going to be all right?" asked the chaplain.

"Yes, I'm OK, sir."

He placed a hand on my shoulder. "Hang in there, Chuck."

"Roger that." I picked up my weapon and headed for the Nissan. My hands were shaking.

Back at the military school barracks, our platoon was eating and getting some rest. I felt a sudden pang of concern for them.

"Stay tactical, men."

Sitting in front of the building, we were listening to President Bush address the nation over the car radio. He announced that there was a new government in Panama, and Noriega was on the run. I leaned against the wall of the school, exhausted but unable to sleep, unable to close my eyes without seeing Lear's face covered in blood. Until now, I had never seen death up close. Until now, death was something that I'd given very little thought to. I guess I felt like most nineteen-year-olds—somewhat invincible. But there in the strengthening sunlight, leaning against the wall of the abandoned military school in a country whose size belied its importance in world affairs, death became very real.

I pulled the dog tags from around my neck and looked at them.

HOLTON, CHARLES W

A POS

And on the bottom line:

BAPTIST

I wondered then why I hadn't just put "Christian" when they asked my religious preference. After all, God's not a Baptist. It's fitting that they put your religion on the bottom line, though, because after all, that *is* the bottom line, really. Five minutes after I die, my blood type and Social Security number won't mean a thing.

The choice that I've made about what to put my faith in will.

14

A Soldier's Christmas

My head throbbed along with the rotor of the MH-53 Pave Low helicopter, thundering west over a seemingly endless triple-canopy jungle. The still-rising tropical sun caused me to squint as its rays penetrated the yawning tailgate of the huge aircraft, piloted by men from the Army's elite Task Force 160.

A crew chief sat on the tailgate, his frame silhouetted in the open rear door and secured to the inside of the chopper by a nylon strap connected to the back of his harness. He leaned on a .50 caliber machine gun mounted in the doorway and watched four more helicopters, visible against a dazzling blue sky as they followed behind us in a staggered formation.

It was Christmas Day, but no one seemed to notice.

I'd not been afforded more than a couple of hours' rest at a time from the day that the invasion began a week earlier, and the two-hour flight presented a needed chance to catch up on some sleep. Slumped on the floor of the aircraft along with the rest of Second Platoon, I was trying to get some shut-eye, but the mission that lay ahead kept running through my mind. Our company was being sent to root out some of Noriega's last remaining forces, who were supposedly holding out in a small town near the Costa Rican border. It was supposed to be a fairly straightforward assignment, but most of us were simply glad to be headed out on mission again.

Every man in the platoon wore yellow foam earplugs to stave off the piercing whine of the twin jet engines mounted on either side of the rotor hub above our heads, making conversation during the flight nearly impossible. Another crewman manned the M-60 machine gun in the chopper's side door just behind the cockpit, wearing an olive drab flight suit of fire-resistant Nomex, and an aviator helmet. The smoke-colored visor covering his face revealed nothing but a firmly set jaw, making him look emotionless, almost inhuman, as he stood in the doorway, scanning for any sign of a threat in the lush tropical foliage scrolling past. I watched as he began talking into the boom microphone attached to his helmet, apparently communicating with the pilots.

Suddenly he went rigid. His right hand flew to the M-60's slide and yanked it back, preparing the weapon to fire. But before he could pull the trigger, the helicopter dropped so sharply that everyone in the aircraft, many of whom had been dozing a second earlier, grabbed for a handhold. I struggled to my feet to get a look at what was causing the alarm.

Peering out the porthole in the side of the aircraft, I was surprised to see ocean beneath us. A backward glance revealed towering cliffs above a rocky coastline and the other helicopters plunging one after another to within fifty feet of the water as soon at they were clear of the breakers. I started to relax as I realized why the chopper had dropped so quickly. Then I almost jumped out of my flak vest as the door gunner to my right opened up with a long burst from the M-60, the sound of it deafening inside the cargo area despite my earplugs.

A week in a combat zone had put us all a little on edge and especially averse to unexpected loud noises. It took me a moment to realize that he was simply test-firing his weapon into the water, and that we were not under attack. I made a conscious effort to breathe deeply to return my heart rate to normal.

A few minutes later we were back over land, flying nap-of-the-earth at treetop level. I staggered over to the open cockpit door and stood bracing myself against the airframe. I had to marvel at the terrain-following radar and ground avoidance radar screens on the console, as well as the skill of the Night Stalker pilots. They made piloting thirty thousand pounds of men and machine five feet above the treetops at one hundred and twenty knots look easier than watching football on television—and a lot more fun.

The pilots were enjoying the chance to put their skills to the test, darting through mountain passes and swooping so low into cleared fields that livestock scattered in fright. It was clear that, like so much else, peacetime flight rules went out the window in combat, replaced by whatever would best shield us from enemy fire. Feeling the adrenaline surge, I was enjoying the ride as well. This was the kind of adventure I'd hoped to find in the Army.

When we parachuted in during the wee hours of December 20, most of us had hoped that we'd be home in a few days, exchanging gifts and spending time with our families. But what had looked like a short and simple operation had dragged on and on, degenerating into a wild-goose chase for Panama's ruthless dictator, Manuel Noriega. Units like ours were scrambling all over this small country looking for the elusive ruler and any forces remaining loyal to him.

Between H-hour and today, we had been sent on several similar missions, which required little more than watching people surrender. Those assignments had taught me a lot. I'd learned that the most frightening part of every operation is the moment before it begins, waiting and wondering while the nervous energy burns in your gut. Once the mission kicks off, however, the part of the brain that was devoted to anxious worry gets diverted to dealing with the here and now, and training takes over.

> I HAD LEARNED THAT VICTORY IS NOT SECURED ON THE BATTLEFIELD, BUT ON THE TRAINING RANGE.

I also learned that the most dangerous part of the "op" is when you think it's over—because it is then that your guard goes down and leaves you most vulnerable to a stupid mistake or a counterattack.

The most *important* lesson that I'd learned, however, is that victory is not secured on the battlefield, but on the training range. So much of the tedium and misery that we'd endured in training was paying big dividends here. It was surprising how instinctive our tactical conduct had become. The night that we jumped in and took the prisoners at Rio Hato, I hadn't even thought about what to do when it came to the room-to-room clearing at the military school. Those actions had been simply automatic.

The hundreds of hours we'd spent doing close-quarters-battle drills, or CQB, paid off when there was only time to react, not think. We hadn't been trying to act brave or aggressive. We were exactly as audacious in combat as we had trained to be in peacetime. I had learned that the battle is won in training, just as the marathon runner's success is determined by the hundreds of training miles leading up to the race.

I'd spent much of the downtime of the last several days evaluating each previous mission, running it over and over in my head, picking it apart to see what I could have done better. Looking back, it was easy to spot not only things that I could improve on, but also the life parallels to these truths.

Just as we needed realistic training to hone our reflexes to the point of automatic response in combat, I couldn't wait until the temptation to sin was upon me to decide how I would react. If I wanted to be successful at making good life choices in the big things, I needed to make consistently wise decisions about the little everyday things. That practice would build in me a foundation of discipline that would win whenever those demons of the flesh came calling.

The time-honored saying "train as you will fight" had proved true once again, in the spiritual realm as well as the physical. It wasn't lost on me that this concept applied to every battle in my life, not just the one here in Panama. My spiritual, emotional, and moral defenses were under attack every day, wherever I happened to be. I needed to analyze my vulnerabilities and think through the trials and temptations that would likely confront my everyday life. Then I could *decide* and *rehearse* ahead of time what my reactions would be—and I'd be better equipped to daily defend my personal integrity.

A simple truth had impressed itself on my mind in the week that we'd been here: Self-discipline—that is, the ability to force oneself to do what must be done—makes the difference between success and failure on *any* battlefield. The better part of discipline—

and victory—is found in training and planning ahead. We'd never have jumped six hundred Rangers onto the airfield at Rio Hato with instructions just to "wing it." We had trained and rehearsed the mission in great detail. Likewise, I can't expect to have the fortitude to make the hard choices in life if I wait until I'm faced with them. My capacity for self-control needs daily training if I want it to be there for me when I need it.

I'd also spent some of our downtime writing letters to my folks, struggling to convey what combat was like. It was tough to describe the feeling of being on a mission, surrounded by pandemonium and uncertainty, in fear of my life and yet shrouded in a driving sense of purpose so powerful that it was almost intoxicating. On one level, the things we were experiencing were uniformly miserable, frenzied, and horrific. Yet the feeling of having a hand in making history, and even more, the chance to finally put to use the hard training that we'd endured made me feel honored to participate in these operations. So many soldiers served out their four years training for the eventuality of combat and never got to see it. We, at least, could say that we'd put our skills into practice.

It was extremely satisfying to watch our training coalesce into victory, to work together as a unit, and to overcome the obstacles set before us.

War is ultimately distasteful, yet at the same time it is somehow glorious. It is *life* boiled down to its most potent and brutal state. And yet, there is a simplicity to it that would be difficult to comprehend for anyone who hasn't seen it firsthand. In combat, everything focuses on the moment. All of life's goals are reduced to one: accomplishing the mission. Life's obstacles and frustrations become incarnate in the forces of the enemy. And most of those obstacles can be overcome by exerting a little over ten pounds of pressure with a trigger finger—something none of us looked forward to.

Combat was the greatest of those experiences that I wouldn't wish on anyone but wouldn't trade for anything.

Now that I'd experienced it firsthand, I fully understood how someone could be completely against war. I hated combat for its brutality, for the horrors that it inflicted on me, yet I understood now better than ever that sometimes sacrifice of this kind is necessary—though the politics behind the war meant little to me at the time. For us, it wasn't some testosterone-produced blood lust that brought us here. We were simply doing our job.

A new understanding of the concept of bravery was taking shape in my head. I had always wondered if I would be brave enough to perform admirably in a combat situation, something that every soldier questions at some point. What I'd realized is that courageous isn't something you are, it's something you do. No one can be called brave until he puts it into practice. Idle courage is no better than revealed cowardice. *Kind of like my faith*, I thought, and James 2:17 came alive in my mind: "Faith by itself, if it is not accompanied by action, is dead."

It wasn't always easy to have faith in our superiors, however. One operation had taken us to a small town called Penonome, where the local penitentiary was suspected to contain some political prisoners. Our regimental commander, Colonel William "Buck" Kernan, had called the prison on the telephone ahead of time and warned them that we were coming. News of this caused quite a stir of discontent among the troops, because none of us was anxious to go into a fight where the enemy had been given ample time to prepare an ambush. We followed orders, however, and when we arrived at the prison, we found Panamanian soldiers standing out front waiting to surrender. The commander's audacious move allowed us to take over the prison without a shot being fired.

Our unit had spent the last several days at Howard Air Force Base, sitting around in a school building that had been appropriated for our use and waiting for something to do. Due to some mistake, the only hot food our cooks had brought along was lasagna, so we ended up eating lasagna two or three meals a day for almost a week. We were excited when this current mission was announced, if for no other reason than getting something different to eat.

The plan was to send about one hundred and thirty of us to the small town of David on the western end of Panama, to secure the airfield there and search for weapons caches and holdout elements of the Panamanian defense forces that were still loyal to Noriega.

As the Pave Low shuddered its way toward our objective, I looked at the faces of the Rangers around me, each one unmistakably familiar despite the ever present Kevlar helmet and thick layer of camouflage makeup. Most of them were dozing off again, seemingly undaunted by the uncertainty that lay ahead. These men were the closest that I would ever come to having brothers. Not that I liked them all the time—I didn't. But in combat, I was glad to be on their team.

Thinking of brothers made me wonder about all the families of these guys. I knew that our participation in Operation Just Cause was harder on our families than it was on us. After all, most of the time we had spent in Panama so far had been quite uneventful. We passed so many hours waiting for something to happen that men started to get anxious for any kind of mission just to break the monotony. Our families had no way of knowing this, however. In their minds we were in mortal danger at every moment. The torture of not knowing what hazards we were facing had to be worse for them than actually facing them was for us.

Fortunately, the first morning after the jump, I had an unusual opportunity to contact my folks. Once most of the shooting had died down, my team had been ordered to secure and hold one corner of a building with attention to the windows facing the jungle. The office that we occupied had only two windows, and there were three of us. So while Chester and Bohannon kept watch, I nosed around the room looking for souvenirs. I spied a telephone on the desk and couldn't resist lifting the receiver. I was surprised to hear a dial tone, since the phone lines were supposed to have been cut. Dialing zero brought a Spanish-speaking operator on the line, and after a few tries I got her to place a collect call to my parents' home in Fort Worth, Texas.

My dad answered on the second ring.

Apparently he'd just been on the other line with my grandmother, assuring her that I probably had nothing to do with the invasion that was on the news. Needless to say, my call came as quite a shock. I assured them that I was safe and then quickly hung up, not wanting them to hear any of the occasional shots still being fired in our area. Until that call, they had been somewhat bewildered as to my sudden disappearance.

Our battalion had been scheduled to go on block leave the morning of December 18, a Monday. The day before, I had stopped by the barracks after church to make sure that my dress uniform was in order, since Jennifer and I had planned to leave for my parents' house in Fort Worth on Monday, as soon as the company got cut loose.

Only I never showed up.

Before I could leave the barracks that Sunday afternoon, the unit was locked down, and all communications with the world outside the green fence that surrounded our compound were forbidden. I knew that Jennifer would have no idea what was going on, but I didn't have any way to contact her. She would be angry with me for not showing up as planned, and then worried when twenty-four hours went by without any word. Although I was extremely busy preparing for the invasion, the fact that I had left her hanging nagged at me constantly.

Now it was Christmas Day, and at this moment my family was probably sitting around in their robes and opening gifts. And here I was sweating in the belly of a cargo helicopter, speeding toward what could be a protracted battle with Noriega's last loyal fighters.

I noticed a spare set of headphones lying on the floor next to the crew chief, plugged into the aircraft's radio system. I donned them quickly, hoping to get more information about our target by listening to the pilots. From listening to the banter between the aircrafts, I picked up that there were two Cobra attack helicopters flying reconnaissance about ten minutes ahead of our formation, and they were radioing back updates. One of the cobras broke in on the net as we neared the objective.

"Be advised, there are over a thousand people on the ground at the objective, possibly hostile, over."

The unforeseen warning hit me like a rifle grenade. This was not in the mission plan. What had been prayers for protection changed instantly to prayers for deliverance.

The door gunner had heard it, too. His jawline took on a grim look as he began preparing extra ammunition for the M-60.

Obviously, we had lost the element of surprise. If the people on the ground were armed, our group of one hundred and thirty

Rangers would be in for a tough time. I turned and relayed the message to the soldiers around me, who passed it on to the rest of the platoon. The cargo area was soon very busy with men performing last-minute checks on weapons and equipment.

"One minute!" the loadmaster shouted, holding up a gloved index finger for those who couldn't hear him. I pulled a magazine out of my ammo pouch and slammed it into the receiver of my M-16, then chambered a round. I then loaded a forty-millimeter buckshot round into the attached grenade launcher, hoping that neither would have to be used.

"Thirty seconds!" I unhooked my safety line from the aircraft, trying not to entertain thoughts that this could be my last Christmas. The man across from me bowed his head and made the sign of the cross. *Amen,* I thought. *God, help us.*

The helicopters swooped into the airfield at full speed, then flared so sharply that the giant aircraft nearly stood on their tails, kicking up a tremendous sandstorm with the rotor wash. We would have fallen right out the open rear door if our forward momentum hadn't been pressing us to the floor. An instant later, the pilots expertly righted the aircraft. I dropped my goggles over my eyes just before stepping off the tailgate of the HH-53 into a windstorm created by its massive eight-bladed rotor disk.

The platoon deployed as quickly as possible, running onto the tarmac in a tight formation with weapons at the ready. The choppers departed as quickly as they had come, shrouding us in chaotic, swirling dust. The cloud settled, revealing several platoons of Rangers, weapons poised, ready for anything.

Anything except this.

The people on the ground weren't enemy soldiers, as we had feared, but the residents of the town. They greeted us with banners and cheers of welcome. We had been expecting a firefight but suddenly found ourselves in a parade. The crowd swarmed toward us, excited and welcoming, as we approached the flight terminal. A couple of our men waved at the cheering throng, while the rest of us didn't quite know what to do.

Staff Sergeant Friar spoke gravely. "This is bad. If there are hostile elements in the crowd and they start shooting at us, we won't be able to engage them without hurting a lot of civilians. Keep on your guard for anyone with a weapon."

Sergeant First Class Kelly must have been thinking the same thing. Just then his voice came over the radio. "Get these people off the airfield—now!"

Since I was one of the few soldiers in my platoon who spoke any Spanish, every squad leader wanted my help at once. I ran around frantically trying to translate for people and get the locals to leave the area. Burdened by my flak vest, Kevlar helmet, and rucksack full of ammo, I soon found myself exhausted and sweating profusely under the tropical sun. My stress meter was pegging out as I hurried from one crisis to another, taxing my limited proficiency in Spanish. The tension increased with each second, as I watched every waving hand for a grenade, being on the lookout for any hostile movement.

Suddenly there was an urgent tugging at the back of my pants leg. I whirled around and raised my rifle, prepared to defend myself, and then froze.

At my feet stood an absolutely beautiful little girl, maybe four years old. Her wide brown eyes looked up at me as she stood petrified with fear. She was barefoot and wore a dusty pink dress.

Her tiny hands trembled as she reached up to hand me something, obviously a gift from her father who was standing nearby.

And at that moment, in the city of David on Christmas Day, I received a most memorable Christmas gift… a small thing, but a big reminder that God still knew right where I was and just what I needed.

It was an ice-cold soda.

Just over two weeks later, several C-141 troop transport planes touched down at Lawson Army Airfield at Fort Benning, Georgia. From them emerged a different group of men than those who had taken off from the same airfield only three weeks earlier. This unit was more mature, having survived its trial by fire. These soldiers looked upon the world with new eyes, having experienced situations that redefined our perception of stress. Having faced death, we had renewed our understanding of what it means to really live.

And apparently we had been missed.

Our battalion marched into the hangar, and there awaiting us were row after row of bleachers filled with friends, loved ones, and the press. After a brief ceremony, we threw ourselves into a ritual practiced in every culture since the beginning of warfare.

Reunion.

Tears, laughter, and frantic hugs and kisses flowed freely as children, wives, parents, and girlfriends rushed to embrace their fathers, husbands, sons, and sweethearts. Jennifer was there, and I hung back momentarily in order to enjoy watching her scan the formation looking for me, savoring the moment of recognition as her face lit up and her eyes grew wide with delight. The relief was tangible between us when we found each other in the crowd and embraced.

In that moment, there was no past, no future. The trauma of the last few weeks and the uncertainty of what was to come melted into the moment as I held her close and realized how much I take for granted in this life.

It was good to be home.

EVERY DAY IS
A NEW BATTLE

For those who fight for it,
life has a flavor the sheltered will never know.
ANONYMOUS

The first morning rays of sunlight filter softly through lace curtains, throwing patterns on the carpet next to my bed. Normally, my cuddly wife and the down comforter combine to create an almost inescapable gravitational pull that threatens to prevent me from ever getting up. But this morning our three-year-old is wedged between us, kicking me in the kidneys, so I throw off the covers and swing my feet to the floor, rubbing the sleep from my eyes.

I stand up and hobble to the door, willing my limbs to work off the usual morning stiffness. I pause at our full-length mirror and have to smile at the lurching spectacle before me, looking more like an old man than I'd like to admit. It's been twelve years since I left the Ranger regiment, and the youthful vigor I possessed then in such abundance has faded, though not completely. (I like to blame my wedding ring for the twenty pounds that I've acquired since then—I joke that the constriction on my finger causes the rest of my body to bloat up.) The soldier is still evident, however, behind the wrinkles and close-cropped hair turning prematurely gray—due more to mileage, I think, than age.

Serving in the Rangers left its mark on me in many ways. I'm an inch shorter than I was in high school, mostly from carrying around that rucksack for four years. That fact bothers me much more than the assortment of battle scars that add character to my frame. The ankle that I broke three weeks before leaving active duty still acts up from time to time. I sound like a bowl of Rice Krispies every morning until my joints get warmed up. But these are a trivial price to pay to join the company of brave soldiers that have served this country since its founding.

This courageous brotherhood knows the price of service. Those who fill its ranks understand that a warrior leads a strategic life—one in which discipline holds a high and honored tradition. They understand the value of belonging to a unit that isn't so much of a team as it is an organism, its members functioning as one body and sharing an intimacy that only soldiers bound by blood can comprehend.

Yes, it's easy to see that the military took its share of my youth, but it's also readily apparent to those who know me that four years as a Ranger brought a mental toughness that was worth the cost. My wife tells single friends, "Find yourself a Ranger to marry. They know how to keep a commitment." The very promise I made to myself when I joined the military—to never quit something because it gets difficult—has helped me in many areas of life, including my marriage. I believe God has honored my commitment to perseverance by allowing me to succeed in most things that I've attempted.

God has continued his practice of blessing me in spite of my own personal failings. My relationship with Jennifer is one example. There came a point, after she and I had been dating for about three years, where I simply was not treating her as well as she deserved, and the relationship was clouding our desire for God's purpose.

Looking back, I see the many ways that God tried to get my attention during this time. But I refused to heed His warnings. I believe that, because of my stubbornness, God simply removed the feelings that Jennifer had for me, and the decline of our relationship was swift and tragic. It was one of the most painful things I've ever experienced.

What is clear now is that God was simply answering the prayers that Rooster and I offered up when Jen and I started dating. Even she and I had prayed that God would be more important to us than we were to each other. And when that stopped being the case, the relationship ended. It's also obvious that He had different plans for my life than I did, plans that turned out to be greater than my wildest dreams.

Since I left the Rangers twelve years ago, God has nearly buried me in blessings. He eventually led me to Connie, a wonderful, godly woman who complements my temperament more perfectly than I ever thought possible. In addition, God has gifted our marriage with five beautiful children, sent specifically to teach me, I believe, what pure joy really is.

The story of my life as a soldier is a wonderful example of God's hand at work. But what's more exciting is the hope that He gives for the future. I'm forever amazed at the adventure He unfolds before me, as I continue to learn and grow under His ever present grace. I've learned that sometimes the hard road is the best one, that joy beats fun any day, and that *who* I am in Christ is much more important than what I do. I've also learned that the pursuit of His purpose is more exciting than fame, fortune, and fantasy taken together.

So how does all this affect you, the reader?

Like I said at the beginning, this isn't meant to be a book about who I've become—it's meant to make you think about who *you* are becoming. I hope that through reading these vignettes about the soldier's life, you've recognized some similarities in your own life. God has an exciting part for you to play in His great plan, but He will use you only as much as you allow Him. Every believer may be a soldier of Christ, but I'm convinced that God is calling us daily to even more. Christ doesn't want to just live in us, but *through* us, to show His purposes to others. To the extent we allow Him to work this way, we can become a more elite solider in His service.

Remember, the elite soldier is a competent, well-trained, well-equipped warrior. While he may not always be privy to the big picture, he understands his portion of the mission and performs it with perseverance and skill, trusting in the knowledge and ability of his commander. When not engaged in combat, he is always training for the next battle.

Being an elite soldier isn't all guns and glory. It is a life of purpose-filled privation, meaningful misery, and postponed payment. It is never easy but always worth it. Pursuing God's purpose is, by definition, the hard road—a path that few will be willing to follow.

The real question is this: Are you willing to be an elite soldier?

Are you ready to allow your Commander to make you more than you were, more than you are, and more than you ever could be without His help? God has a special mission for each of us, and for this reason we were given our few moments on earth. So don't be afraid. Join the battle!

Time is short, and the mission cannot wait.

Even today, I still feel like a warrior on active duty—only now the assignments I'm carrying out aren't merely of political or even historic importance. These operations have eternal ramifications, and that knowledge gives me the driven, focused purpose that comes with the call to battle.

Every day is a new battle, and this is no training exercise.

Once again, I'm on mission.

THE STORY
BEHIND THE STORY

In 1999 I felt compelled to start a website for teens. I wrote weekly articles and posted them there. After a few months, I started getting e-mails encouraging me to get some of the articles published. I've been a writer since I was fourteen, keeping journals throughout my teens and twenties. That had been mostly a therapeutic exercise... until recently.

One night I awoke in the midst of a dream about the invasion of Panama. Shaken by the memory, I stumbled downstairs and wrote what became the prologue of this book. After posting it on Mission4me.com, the response was fantastic, and everyone had the same question: "What happened next?"

Shortly thereafter, my wife, Connie, who is the librarian for our church, wanted some humorous reading to add to the collection. She discovered Dave Meurer's book *Daze of Our Wives,* and she laughed so hard that I had to read the book myself. Eventually, I e-mailed Dave to ask him how he had become a writer. Dave was kind enough to answer my questions, and later he read my account of the jump into Panama. He encouraged me to attend the Mount Hermon Christian Writers Conference in California that spring. I'd never met Dave, but I took his advice and sent in my registration.

At the conference I submitted my Panama story to Multnomah Publishers, mostly because one of my favorite authors, Randy Alcorn, writes for them. One of their editors, Judy Gordon, liked what she saw and requested that I send a formal book proposal. There it might have died in committee—except for a timely meeting. Bill Jensen, the vice president of editorial, was scheduled to be in the Washington, D. C., area where I live, and Judy convinced him to meet with me. Bill and I talked over pancakes one morning, and he returned to Oregon as an advocate for my book.

The book prevailed in meeting after meeting. In September 2002 I flew to Oregon for a backpacking trip and also visited the Multnomah offices. I met people throughout the company, and all were warm and welcoming. Then through an unusual series of events, I ended up having dinner that evening at the home of Don Jacobson, the president of Multnomah. Several weeks later I received a contract.

I appreciate all of you who have been a part of this adventure. Connie has been a constant encouragement, even when that meant becoming a writer's widow during the four months that I pounded out the majority of the manuscript. And this book would have never made it out of my head had it not been for the intense prayer support of many, including my parents, Mike and Kathy Holton, and my accountability partner, Graham Davis. My good friend Dean Peters takes time out from Blogs4God.com to help me keep my own website up and running. Many other friends from my church and around the country have prayed with me over this project, and my friend and fellow writer Lynne Thompson has been a great source of advice. In addition, Naomi Linn, a wonderful octogenarian who spent forty years as a copy editor, pre-edited all of the chapters before they went to my editor, Judy, at Multnomah.

Most of all, however, I am grateful to the One who saw me through the dangers of my youth, called me to His service, and gave me the wonderful family of fellow believers mentioned above. May God use this work as a recruiting tool for His kingdom, guiding them to Him, my source of daily joy.

These days, Chuck Holton spends his time writing, farming, and raising children on his small farm in Maryland. In addition, he enjoys pursuing the important and exciting mission of ministering to teens across the country through speaking and wilderness survival trips.

If you'd like to know more about becoming an elite soldier in God's army, you can e-mail Chuck directly at:
chuck@moreelitesoldier.com

The publisher and author would love to hear your comments about this book. *Please contact us at:*
www.multnomah.net/chuckholton